BULFINCH ARCHITECTURE/TRAVEL SERIES

AN ARCHITECT'S

Rome

AN ARC

BULFINCH ARCHITECTURE/TRAVEL SERIES

HITECT'S

Rome

John M. McGuire, Jr.

A BULFINCH PRESS BOOK

Little, Brown and Company

Boston   New York   Toronto   London

Acknowledgments

Much of this book finds its roots in the Edinburgh College of Art where I studied and taught from 1985 to 1987. I am greatly indebted to Colin McWilliam from whom I learned to see cities as living records of human endeavor. I am sorry he is not here to share in the writing of this book.

I would like to thank the editors at Bulfinch Press: Brian Hotchkiss for his support and conviction that what I had to say about cities mattered, and Karen Dane and Sue Betz, who served as model editors, respected the work, and helped hone the writing.

My sons, Chris and Tim, have provided both inspiration and their own insights throughout the writing of this book. They too have taught me how to see and enjoy a city. At times it was at their urgings that some wonderful place has been discovered.

Above all, I am grateful to my wife, Brenda, whose ideas and wisdom are as much a part of this work as my own.

Library of Congress Cataloging-in-Publication Data

McGuire, John M., 1949–
    An architect's Rome / John M. McGuire, Jr. — 1st ed.
      p.   cm. — (Bulfinch architecture/travel series)
    ISBN 0-8212-1954-5
    1. Architecture—Italy—Rome—Themes, motives.   2. Rome (Italy)—
Buildings, structures, etc.—Guidebooks.   3. Rome (Italy)—
Guidebooks.   I. Title.   II. Series.
NA1120.M45   1994
720′.945′632—dc20   94-1268

Bulfinch Press is an imprint and trademark of
Little, Brown and Company (Inc.)
Published simultaneously in Canada by
Little, Brown & Company (Canada) Limited

PRINTED IN HONG KONG

To Brenda

Santa Maria della Pace

Contents

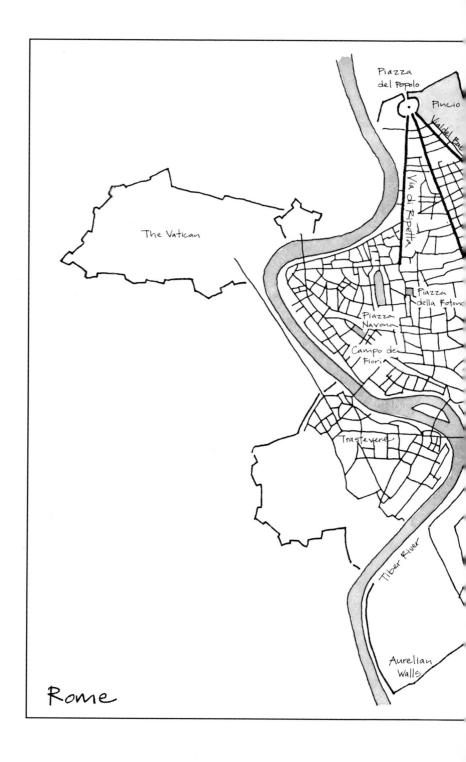

Rome

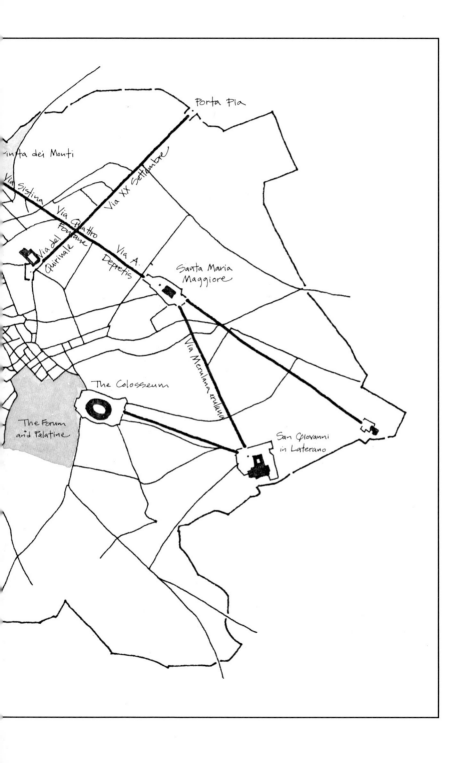

Arch
Campidoglio

Author's Note

Rome, the city, is a work of architecture. Rome is not a museum, but is a vibrant and dynamic city—a place where we encounter Classical ruins next to the elegant facades of Renaissance buildings. Rome is where we find heavy stone medieval buildings next to sleek Modern buildings. In such a city we find important works by famous artists and architects and less famous works by those who just simply planted a garden or built a gate.

What makes Rome special to me is my understanding of the history of the city, knowing who died where and who said what. These writings do not intend to cover every aspect of the city. Rome after all has a history that is nearly thirty centuries old. The book examines "pieces" of the city: some famous, some not; some large, some not. Through the book we visit a selection of Rome's most public places, and we find many of Rome's most secret places. All in an effort to understand what this great city is all about—its character, its mood, its feeling—the world city and the ordinary city. To further this understanding, the book links up many aspects of Rome's history as it relates to the city as a work of architecture.

Roman Forum

Much of my travelling is with friends, family, or architecture students whom I teach while in Europe during the summer. Most of my travel experiences are shared. These are the experiences I would like to share with you, the reader. This small glimpse of Rome includes you. As I write, we are travelling together. With a few exceptions, where I am relying on my memory, we will see and experience Rome during the summer of 1993. That summer was one of the hottest and driest on record, with nearly three months without rain.

I took up residence at the Pensione Parlamento, just off the Corso. The hotel was a warm and friendly place, where Daniela and Plinio (the owners) made every effort to welcome their guests to Rome. In the morning, the ringing of the bells of San Silvestro would signal the beginning of the day. A visit to one of the local cafés would start the activities of most days. I would spend much of the morning exploring the city and drawing. After a light lunch, I would return "home" for the afternoon siesta and a visit with Plinio. We would talk about everything from Rome's staggering collection of art to the impossible heat of the Roman summer. In the coolness of the early evening I would sit on the roof terrace—overlooking the Piazza San Silvestro below—and write in my journal. After dinner, if with a friend, we would usually visit one of our favorite gelato shops and talk away the warm Roman summer night, or, if alone, I might just enjoy the sights and sounds of the evening and watch the parade of people pass by.

Some of my exploration was deliberate; some was not. Along these walks I would stop and take time to fill the pages of my journal and describe the places that interested me. Both the text and the drawings are the notes from these places. The drawings in particular are about seeing and remembering the place. Once your eye has guided your pen along the edge of a building or has examined how the sunlight reveals the detail of an Ionic capital, you have experienced the place and it becomes a part of you.

The walks that the book takes are organized to meander along the roads set out by Pope Sixtus V in the sixteenth century. These streets were laid out in a manner that gave Rome a system of broad straight streets that provided Rome with the townscape it has today. As we follow along the Sistine routes, the city's history reveals itself.

In this book Rome is seen as an important world city and as an everyday city, a place to live and to work. A place for children to play, and a place to picnic in the park.

Rome's Townscape: *Discovering Rome*

> *. . . so majestic as to promise well from this beginning how*
> *many marvels must lie within so famous a city.*
>
> *Anonymous Italian author,*
> *describing the impression Rome makes upon*
> *the traveller*
> *1686*

For many of us Rome is a city of memory. We know the Colosseum and the Forum belong to Rome. We know that the pope, supreme spiritual head of the Catholic Church, resides in the Vatican. We know Michelangelo, Raphael, and Bernini did some of their finest work in Rome. And we know *La Dolce Vita*, which described life in Rome as a life filled with cafés and cappuccinos and as a carefree life that allowed bathing in the Trevi Fountain. It is with these memories that we arrive in the Eternal City.

The city of Rome has its legendary beginnings on the Palatine (one of the original seven hills) some thirty centuries ago. Today Rome stretches from Tivoli, in the hills to the east, to Ostia, on the sea to the west. Rome belongs to no single historical period, and within each of the different neighborhoods, ancient, medieval, Renaissance, and recent buildings stand side by side. All great cities possess a character that makes them more than just a collection of buildings. This character, first and foremost, is expressed by the layout of the streets. The streets organize and guide the development of these cities. The streets reveal these cities to us. The life of such cities, the celebrations as well as the everyday occurrences, is imprinted on the streets. These are the cities that are themselves works of art.

Via Appia Antica

When Sixtus V was elected Pope in 1585 there was only one example which fit his vision of what the new Rome, the Capitol of Christendom, might be like—Michelangelo's design for the Campidoglio. The rest of Rome was a jumbled medieval city covering only one-third of the area within the Aurelian Walls, and the Pope's aim was to extend the inhabited areas of the city to these walls. This was a tremendously ambitious plan, since Rome's population was only one hundred thousand inhabitants.

Pope Sixtus V's plan was quite ingenious and yet quite simple. His plan called for the extension of a series of straight streets to interconnect the important city gates and monuments—including five of the city's seven pilgrimage churches—which lay in the empty space between the city wall and the medieval city. This single act raised Rome out of chaos and provided the city with the most significant element of its townscape: the long uninterrupted vista anchored by an important monument or public space.

From the city's main entrance in the northern wall, Porta del Popolo, three streets radiate. Via di Ripetta leads to where the ancient harbor, the Porto di Ripetta, once stood. Via Flaminia, the present-day Via del Corso, leads to the Capitol and the Forum, and Via del Babuino leads to the Spanish Steps. In the original plan a fourth street, just to the north of Via del Babuino, was to have led to the church Trinità dei Monti at the top of the Spanish Steps.

The principal cross street, named both Via del Quirinale and Via XX Settembre, runs between Michelangelo's entrance to the city, the Porta Pia, in the eastern wall to the statues of the *Dioscuri (Horse Tamers)* on the Quirinal Hill. To assure a visual connection would be made between these two monuments, Pope Sixtus V lowered the grade of this street by as much as four feet. From the church Santa Maria Maggiore now in central Rome, two streets branch off to the southeast: one to Santa Croce and the other to San Giovanni in Laterano. To complete the network of streets, another street leads from San Giovanni to the Colosseum.

To emphasize the long vistas created by the new streets, Sixtus V placed obelisks at terminal points. He placed one of his obelisks to greet visitors as they arrived at the city's principal gate, Porta del Popolo. Later on, this obelisk was to provide the focus for the further development of the surrounding piazza. A second obelisk was placed at the west end of the church Santa Maria Maggiore. A third obelisk stands in front of St. Peter's, and a fourth stands in front of San Giovanni in Laterano. The four obelisks Pope Sixtus V placed, along with his new straight streets, gave order to Rome's existing monuments and columns and gave direction to the city's future development.

The design of the buildings that followed was influenced by Pope Sixtus V's overall design. The new buildings lined the new streets and en-closed the open spaces defined by the obelisks. Pope Sixtus V's idea, more than any other, dominates the visual image — the townscape — of Rome. Sixtus V died in 1590, well before his new city design was completed at the end of the seventeenth century.

For the most part the Aurelian Walls define the center of the city and the area most visited. To understand this area, the area contained by the Aurelian Walls, you must experience the city herself and discover the piazzas, cloisters, fountains, and cafés firsthand. The best way to discover

Rome

Rome is to let the streets of the popes guide and serve as reference points as you follow your instincts and find what lies "just around the corner." Rome is an introverted and secretive place that hides its treasures. To discover these treasures all you need to do is wander. While on your journey, make sure that every once in a while you explore one of the many narrow dark streets which are often the coolest places in the heat of the summer. In these streets lie the discovery of quiet cloisters, serene palm-covered gardens, and ancient columns holding secrets from the past.

Walks: *The Streets of the Popes*

*A good traveler does not, I think, much mind the uninteresting
places. He is there to be inside them, as a thread is inside the
necklace it strings. The world, with unknown and unexpected
variety, is a part of his own Leisure; and this living
participation is, I think, what separates the traveler and the
tourist, who remains separate, as if he were at the theater, and
not himself a part of whatever the show may be.*

Freya Stark
Alexander's Path (*1958*)

From Piazza del Popolo

The Piazza del Popolo serves as the starting point for a series of walks. The
streets that radiate from the piazza give the initial direction. Then curiosity
draws us away from the main street to narrower, quieter passages, where
small shops, little galleries, as well as artisans' studios, hide from the more
tourist-oriented street.

"Nothing in Piazza del Popolo gives the magnificent impression
of Rome better than this initial view, which strikes the visitor at the moment of arrival." This is how Charles de Brosses described his arrival when
writing his *Lettres familières écrites d'Italie en 1739 et 1740.*

Today when we arrive in Rome we can enter the city in a variety
of ways. We can arrive by plane at Rome's airport in Fiumicino, then take
a taxi or the Metropolitana (Rome's subway) to our destination in the city.
We can arrive by train or bus and find ourselves at the Termini in the heart
of the city. Or we can drive into the city from any of the highways which
lead to Rome.

For centuries, though, most travellers arrived from the north on
the Via Flaminia, one of Rome's oldest consular roads. Entering the city at

the Porta del Popolo, the Piazza del Popolo was the first impression they would have had of the city. It is here that the full force of Pope Sixtus V's street design is realized. In a city of many beautiful piazzas, Piazza del Popolo is among the finest. As we pass under the city gate, the piazza swirls in front of us. In the center of the piazza, surrounded by speeding cars, stands Rome's second-oldest obelisk. Dating from the thirteenth century B.C. and brought to Rome from Heliopolis by Augustus, it was moved to the piazza from the Circus Maximus in 1589.

From the obelisk radiates Giuseppe Valadier's great sweeping *exedrae*, large semicircular niches, which enclose two sides of the piazza. Just beyond the edge of the great oval piazza, where the three streets fan out, stand the twin churches of Santa Maria dei Miracoli and Santa Maria di Monte Santo. These churches frame the most dramatic views into the city and remind us that we have finally arrived in Rome.

It is from here, under the arch of the gate, that the fantastic architectural perspectives used in Italian Renaissance theater can be seen, only this time the proscenium is formed by the two churches, which appear to be identical. In 1660 Carlo Rainaldi was commissioned to design the twin churches, and it was determined that they would have to be identical in order to achieve the full potential of the site and provide the architectural introduction to the city. Rainaldi was presented with a very difficult problem—the two sites were of different widths. This is where Rainaldi's genius is revealed. The Santa Maria di Monte Santo, located on the narrower site to the left, was given an oval dome, while the dome of the Santa Maria dei Miracoli, to the right, is round, thus preserving the appearance of symmetry. With the help of both Gian Lorenzo Bernini and Carlo Fontana, the two churches were finally completed in 1679.

Santa Maria del Popolo is barely visible from the square. Its entrance, immediately to our left as we enter the city from the Porta del Popolo, is all but buried behind the new buildings constructed over the past three hundred years during the evolution of the piazza. Most of the church's adjacent monastery was cleared out to make way for the approach to the Pincio Gardens. This is the church that John Ruskin considered the "most perfectly finished," second only to St. Peter's. Most of Rome's

Piazza del Popolo

important artists have work here—Bramante, Bernini, Raphael, Caravaggio—and the great works in the little church include Pinturicchio's frescoes located above the high altar. (The church is badly lit, so take the time to turn on the lights. The switch is just above the balustrade to the left.)

The architectural jewel of the church is the Cappella Chigi. Agostino Chigi, a wealthy banker from Siena and Raphael's friend and patron, asked him to design a chapel "to convert earthly things into heavenly." To achieve this, Raphael designed a miniature church, a church within a church. The mosaics in the dome of the little church are beautiful and mystical. The Venetian tileworker Luigi di Pace executed Raphael's designs in rich hues of blue set in gold. In the design we can see what, for its time, was a curious mixture of both sacred and profane elements. We see God the Father surrounded by the sun and the planets.

This juxtaposition is made all the more interesting after seeing the monument to G. B. Gisleni near the front door. At the top we see a portrait of Gisleni as he was in life, with the inscription NEITHER LIVING HERE. Below this portrait is a gruesome yellow skeleton with the inscrip-

tion NOR DEAD HERE. Between the two are a chrysalis and a butterfly as the symbol of resurrection. It was unusual to associate the afterlife with the emergence of a butterfly from the chrysalis. Santa Maria del Popolo is where Martin Luther worshiped in 1511 before he was excommunicated for claiming that any person could talk directly to God without having to pay a priest.

To the east of the piazza a series of graceful ramps and stairways cascade down from the beautiful Pincio Gardens (all designed by Valadier) to the Piazza del Popolo, where a bubbling little fountain by Carlo Maderno is placed. This is matched on the opposite side by Carlo Fontana's fountain, which is framed by a small grove of trees.

The Piazza del Popolo remains the trendy place to meet after an evening drive or the place to sip a cappuccino after shopping in the surrounding shops. When one of the local sports teams is victorious, the piazza is the scene of wild celebration. In the quiet of the morning children can be found playing on the eccentric lion water fountains that surround the obelisk of Rameses II.

Along Via del Babuino

Via del Babuino

Leaving Piazza del Popolo by the southeasterly Via del Babuino, we soon leave behind the bustle of the square. This is a quiet street lined with small shops, mostly bookstores or upmarket clothing stores, along with some of the city's finest art galleries. After a leisurely walk, visiting several of the shops along the way, we arrive at Rome's most popular spot, the Piazza di Spagna, and what is perhaps the most famous pedestrian "street" in the world, the Spanish Steps. Here we are in the Rome of the foreigners, a Rome only about three hundred years old. Because of all the English who made the area around the piazza their home while in Rome, the area became known as the English Ghetto. On the Grand Tour the lords and ladies, as well as the artists of Europe, were all drawn to the Eternal City: Robert Adam, Stendhal, Balzac, Hans Christian Andersen, Rubens, Tennyson, Poussin, Liszt, Wagner, Byron. And especially Keats, who died in February of 1821, with a gentle smile on his lips, in a small room looking out onto the sunlit spaces of the Spanish Steps.

The first time I came to Rome I asked for a map of the city at the hotel where I was staying. With great fanfare about the virtues of the location of the hotel, I was presented a map which was promptly opened by the proprietor who circled both the location of my hotel and the Spanish Steps, my only two necessary points of reference. The Steps, which flow down from the twin towers of Trinità dei Monti, were constructed with the monies left by the French ambassador Etienne Gueffier when he died in 1660. Gueffier left these funds to build a chapel in Trinità dei Monti and a stair to replace the muddy tree-lined path that then led to the church. The wide sweeping stairs climb gently to broad landings. On any evening the Steps are a place of rendezvous for people of all ages from around the world. Charles Dickens observed that the faces of the people who gathered on the Steps were the faces he had encountered on the canvases exhibited across Europe. The Spanish Steps provide a place for all those coming to Rome seeking inspiration.

Probably the most interesting building on the piazza is the huge Palazzo di Propaganda Fide, located at the narrow south end of the piazza. This was an institution founded by Pope Gregory XV in 1622. The exterior of the palazzo is the joint work of the two architects Gian Lorenzo Bernini and Francesco Borromini. Their rivalry is clearly evident here. On the Via di Propaganda we can see the concave and convex windows begun in 1650 by Borromini, and on the piazza facade we can see the more dignified work of Bernini completed in 1644. Standing before the palace is an enormous column supporting a statue of the Virgin. This is the object that guided us as we left Piazza del Popolo and forms the link back to the obelisk in the center of the piazza.

The Fontana della Barcaccia (literally the Fountain of the Worthless Boat) is one of the city's most clever fountains. The "old barge" sits at the foot of the Spanish Steps, sinking into a shallow pool of water. Whether he was inspired by a boat actually deposited on land after a flood or, more pragmatically, was accommodating low water pressure, Bernini (it is still uncertain whether it is the work of the father or the son) designed the fountain so that the water flows slowly from the bow and the stern of the boat into a shallow pool. This is the perfect place to watch hundreds of people pass by while you sit and enjoy the fountain at the foot of these great steps.

Soaring high above the Spanish Steps is the church of Trinità dei Monti. The facade and the twin belfries are the work of Carlo Maderno, the same architect who was responsible for the facade of St. Peter's. One of the most picturesque images in all of Rome is the composition of the fountain of the "old barge" and the meandering flow of the Spanish Steps with their Roman obelisk leading to the twin belfries of Trinità dei Monti rising into the sky.

Now to climb those steps, a flight of stairs broken by a series of three large landings, which allow for a gentle climb with ample time to pause and enjoy the view as we rise above the piazza. If you are lucky enough to visit Rome in May or June, you will be able to make your climb among huge vases of azaleas. The fragrance from this waterfall of blooms is nearly overwhelming. The view from the top overlooking the Spanish Steps is almost as dramatic as looking up from below. With the obelisk in the foreground, we can see the Via Condotti running toward the Tiber.

Before we leave the hill there are two other interesting places to

Spanish Steps

Palazzetto Zuccari

visit. To the south, just around the corner on Via Gregoriana, is the house built by the artist Federico Zuccari. What is curious about this house is that the main entrance and the windows are carved to represent the faces of monsters, with their mouths forming the opening for either a door or a window. It is here that the Swiss painter Angelica Kauffmann lived in the eighteenth century.

To the north, along the Viale Trinità dei Monti, is the austere Villa Medici, where Galileo was imprisoned from 1630 to 1633 by order of the Inquisition, which is now the home of the French Academy.

After a morning of exploring the area around the Spanish Steps it is time to do a little less deliberate sightseeing. Leading out of the piazza toward the west is the Via Condotti. This is the most fashionable street in the heart of Rome's shopping district. If shopping is not the ticket, then the Caffè Greco (number 86) is a terrific place for coffee or a light lunch. After all, Goethe, Wagner, and Hemingway once visited these elegant rooms filled with paintings. Elizabeth Barrett Browning met Hans Christian Andersen here. Who will gather here today?

Via del Corso

For our journey let's begin at the obelisk in the center of the Piazza del Popolo. Looking down Via del Corso, we see the giant columns of the Monumento Vittorio Emanuele just visible in the rising heat of midday. As we begin our walk down the Corso, we pass between the Santa Maria dei Miracoli and the Santa Maria di Monte Santo. Walking out of the midday sun into the shade of the churches, the temperature immediately drops fifteen degrees Fahrenheit. At this point the street is narrow, only about thirty feet wide.

Just past the house where Goethe stayed (number 20), the first building of significance we come to is the Ospedale San Giacomo, founded in 1339. Within the hospital is Francesco da Volterra's church, San Giacomo degli Incurabili, built in 1590. This church has a very early elliptical plan, emphasizing the long axis that terminates at the high altar. In this church we can see the simple beginnings of what would become dynamic Baroque architecture late in the seventeenth century. The street running next to San Giacomo, the Via Antonio Canova, is named after the famous sculptor who lived there. Number 17, Antonio Canova's studio, is covered with fragments of Classical sculpture and has a bronze bust of the artist embedded in the wall.

Just before we reach the intersection at Via Condotti we arrive at the "little room" in front of the church, Largo San Carlo al Corso. This "little room" is created by the church being pulled back at a slight angle from the street, forming an irregular space outside in front of the church. This is the church with the gleaming cream-colored facade. It is more widely known for the magnificent dome that cascades down to Piazza Augusto. The dome is Pietro da Cortona's last masterpiece, built in 1668–72. The dome is beautiful as part of Rome's skyline, but it is at the street where the church really belongs to the city. The broad steps of the church flow out away from the entrance and into the street to provide a special place along the Corso to pause. During any time of the day, but particularly in the evening when the street is full of people shopping or just out for the evening promenade, the steps are always occupied. This is the perfect place to rest with the children after visiting the enormous toy shop, Galleria San Carlo, across the street.

The Corso used to be the main street for elegant shops. To understand what the great shops along the Corso must have been like, there are three historic shops that are reminiscent of the heady days of the Corso. Masenza and Cravanzola are elegant jewelry shops full of polished wood shelves covered with sparkling silver. And the famous Attanasio specializes in antique watches and clocks of all sorts.

The Via Condotti is next. Via Condotti, the finest shopping street in this district, climbs gently up to the Piazza di Spagna. It is at this intersection that Pope Sixtus V's street plan comes alive, and we can experience what the Sistine plan of Rome intended to do. From here on the Corso our view up Via Condotti takes us to the Piazza di Spagna, up the Spanish Steps, around the obelisk, right up to the twin towers of the Trinità dei Monti, standing on the skyline. Back to our left is the obelisk placed in the center of Piazza del Popolo. This intersection, where Via Condotti crosses the Corso, is one of those special places where one can see two of

Largo San Carlo al Corso

the obelisks used to organize the city. By understanding connections through movement and vistas, we begin to appreciate and experience Rome.

At one o'clock in the morning, when warm Roman nights are still young, the auto races begin down the Corso at the traffic signal on the Via di Convertite. Just past this intersection is the Piazza Colonna. This is one of the most famous squares in the city. The beginnings of Piazza Colonna

Near Piazza Colonna

are connected to the extravagant celebrations of the Carnival, which took place on the Via del Corso starting in the fifteenth century. When the Corso became the place of horse races and parades, the once lower-class residential area began to transform into an elegant district where upper-class Romans came for their evening stroll.

The Column of Marcus Aurelius, which now dominates the piazza, stood alone in the midst of medieval tenements until the sixteenth century, when the Palazzo Ferraioli along the south was built. In 1580 Giacomo della Porta began construction on the Palazzo Chigi (now the seat of the Presidency of the Council of Ministers) along the north side of the piazza. Eventually the Palazzo Wedekind (1838) and, across the Corso, the Galleria Colonna (1923) were built to complete all four sides of the square.

The Column of Marcus Aurelius commemorates the victorious battles against the Sarmathians and the Marcomanni. Originally erected in the Campus Martius between A.D. 180 and 196, the column depicts Marcus Aurelius fifty-nine times, but not one of the reliefs shows him in battle. And today, instead of a statue of Marcus Aurelius on top of the column, we find Domenico Fontana's statue of St. Paul, which was placed there in 1589.

In the eighteenth century the base of this important monument to Roman culture was surrounded by dozens of coffee-roasting ovens that burned around the clock to produce the valuable roasted beans for the city. Due to a local law that regulated where various trades could be located within the city, and because of the aroma of the roasting beans, the piazza was designated as the only place where the coffee roasters could work. All of this is now only a memory, but on quiet mornings it is possible to imagine the piazza as the "coffee shop" to the city. When Rome became the capital of Italy toward the end of the nineteenth century, the piazza became a commercial and political center. Coffee roasting was abandoned in favor of bands playing the popular songs of the day. The surrounding bars and cafés catered to the rich and famous, while the piazza was always full of grand horse-drawn carriages.

Behind Piazza Colonna, to the west, is the Piazza di Montecitorio, which serves as the main entrance to the Palazzo di Montecitorio. The large palazzo was originally designed by Bernini in 1650 for Pope Innocent X to house the papal tribune. The facade, with its giant pilasters that embrace the upper stories, is entirely the work of Bernini. Carlo Fontana, who completed the work in 1694, is responsible for the entrance and the campanile above the clock. Since 1871 the palazzo has been the seat of the Italian Chamber of Deputies, the lower house of the Italian Parliament. The real treasure of the palazzo lies inside. When the Parliament is not in session the elegant semicircular Art Nouveau hall is open to the public. It is in this beautiful room, designed by Ernesto Basile in 1918, that many of Italy's political debates have taken place.

In the center of Piazza di Montecitorio, directly in front of the palazzo, stands another obelisk. It is the fourth largest of the thirteen found in Rome today. There were forty-eight obelisks that stood in Rome during classical times. Brought by Augustus from Heliopolis, the Obelisk of Psammetichus II was originally erected as the gnomon, or shaft, for the great sundial in the Campus Martius. The red granite monolith was recovered in the time of Sixtus V, but not placed in the piazza until the end of the seventeenth century. Originally all of the obelisks in Rome had a gnomon and ball, which enabled them to accurately cast a shadow and function as sundials. Today all of the obelisks but two, this one and the one at Villa Mattei, have had the gnomon and ball replaced by a cross. The ancient sundial, the Obelisk of Psammetichus II, marks the place most favored by tourists to photograph the sober entrance to the palazzo. It also serves as the place from which to shout, to all of those who will listen, whatever complaint or advice one may have concerning the government.

From here I suggest we take the Via degli Uffici del Vicario to the Pantheon. Via degli Uffici del Vicario is a narrow street leading away from the Piazza di Montecitorio. At number 40 we will find Giolitti, the most famous Roman ice-cream shop in the city. The ice cream is excellent, and the range of choices daunting. A little farther along on the Via della Maddalena, the street leading to the Pantheon, we find Bar Viola. Here we have every variety of chocolate imaginable. When we reach the Piazza di Maddalena we discover the exquisite little church of Santa Maria Maddalena with its undulating cream-colored facade, broken cornices, and stucco niches filled with statues. This is one of the few examples of Roman Rococo. And finally on the Via del Pantheon is Fiocco di neve, famous for its homemade ice cream.

PLAN

Figure-ground showing the public spaces
around the Pantheon

1.
Piazza di Maddalena

2.

Santa Maria Maddalena

3.

Via del Pantheon

4.

Via del Pantheon

5.

Piazza della Rotonda

Piazza della Rotonda   This morning we visit the Piazza della Rotonda. Sitting with a cappuccino and gazing at the Pantheon with its dome and its massive columns—like a grove of fat trees holding up the porch—is one of the best ways to spend Sunday morning. The piazza is still quiet; only the sound of the choir singing under that great dome can be heard. The great dome was described in 1549 by William Thomas in his *History of Italy* as "vaulted like the half of an egg." The Pantheon has been the most admired monument in Rome for nearly two thousand years. In spite of Agrippa's inscription (implying that he was responsible for the construction of the Pantheon), we now know that the Pantheon was built in the ancient Campus Martius during the reign of Hadrian. The porch is supported by sixteen monolithic Corinthian columns carved from gray and red Egyptian granite. The *cella* (sanctuary) is roofed with what was, until this century, the largest dome, with a diameter of 142 feet. The wonderful sense of harmony and balance is achieved by the relationship between the diameter of the dome and the height of the building. The dimensions of the diameter of the dome and the height of the building are equal and are based on the geometry of a circle.

Hadrian was an engineer of the first order. The coffered ceiling of the dome reveals its structure, which is there for all to see. The ribs between the coffers show exactly how the loads of the dome are transmitted to the walls. The thickness of the dome diminishes from 19 feet 4 inches at the base to 4 feet 10 inches at the oculus. The oculus is 29 feet 3 inches in diameter. Originally ringed with bronze, the oculus lights the interior space from above. In ancient times, before the sheets were plundered, the roof of the dome was covered with sheets of gilded bronze. It was the bronze from the beams in the portico that was used for the *baldacchino* (ornamental canopy) in St. Peter's. The great bronze doors at the entrance are the largest of the surviving bronze doors in Rome.

Such a building would seem to overwhelm all those who enter. Instead there is a comfortable feeling, an almost human quality, about this ancient structure. In the Pantheon we can sense the calm and magical spirit of the classical world. The quality of the light that streams in from above and reveals each niche is the most important element of the Pantheon.

There is enough light to illuminate the entire space. The light is always moving, and it is natural. This light enters only through the unglazed opening of the oculus above us. It is in this natural light that we see the simple interior. This is where Raphael sleeps.

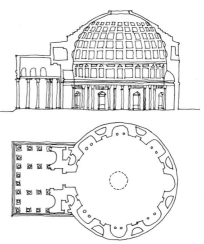

The Pantheon

After the Fall of Rome, the Byzantine emperor Phocas presented the building to Boniface IV, who then consecrated it as a Christian church in 609. This is probably the single most important act that saved the Pantheon from destruction. Today the Pantheon is a Christian church, entombing Raphael and two Italian kings, Victor Emmanuel II and Umberto I.

It is hard to imagine that in the Piazza della Rotonda, which contains the Pantheon and one of Rome's fine Renaissance fountains serving as the base for Rameses II's obelisk, the city's fish market flourished until 1847. I think the piazza is much better suited as a place to sit and gaze at the great Rotonda and contemplate all that is beautiful. If contemplation is not in order and you are in the mood for coffee, then the famous Tazza d'Oro can offer you the best cup of coffee in Rome.

Immediately behind the Pantheon is the Piazza della Minerva. Standing in front of the church Santa Maria sopra Minerva, in the midst of parked cars, is Bernini's famous elephant upon whose back is mounted another obelisk. The Minerva, as it is commonly known, is the only Gothic church in the city. Do not expect, though, the towering Gothic church typical of northern Europe. The present church dates from 1280, when it was designed by two Dominican monks, Friars Sisto and Ristoro. These monks also designed the interior of the famous church Santa Maria Novella in Florence. The facade is rather plain by Gothic standards, and the interior still retains its austere Italian Gothic quality after more than seven hundred years.

Sant' Ivo

Inside we find the wonderful frescoes in the Cappella Caraffa by Filippino Lippi, Michelangelo's statue *The Redeemer*, the Tomb of Guillaume Durand (1296) by Giovanni Cosmati, and a little-known work by Bernini, the Monument to Maria Ruggi. I was unexpectedly struck by the beautiful and remarkable work of the tomb of St. Catherine of Siena, one of Italy's national saints. The expression on her face is absolutely captivating. St. Catherine of Siena was the mystically inspired Dominican sister who was largely responsible for the papacy's return to Rome from Avignon. When she died, the room in which she died was moved in total to the sacristy of the Minerva. To commemorate her death, the popes came in a solemn procession on the Feast of the Annunciation each year until 1870.

To our left as we leave Santa Maria sopra Minerva is the Holiday Inn, a hotel on the grand scale. In the early evening, the bar and restaurant on the roof garden is a quiet place to come for refreshments or dinner. From the roof garden one can look across the red-tiled roofs spiked with television antennae, across the buildings cloaked in faded Roman stucco, and see the dome of St. Peter's. Rising out of the jumble of buildings is the

Monument to Victor Emmanuel II, and we can see beyond to the hills surrounding the city. But sitting right in front of us is the twisted lantern of Borromini's Sant'Ivo.

While we sit on the roof and sip our *granita*, a cool ice drink, our thoughts turn to Borromini, the architect of that strange twisted lantern which is probably the oddest in all of Rome. Borromini had a humble beginning, starting his work life as a stonemason. At fifteen he worked on the stonework for St. Peter's. For years he worked under Bernini. In 1634, when he was nearly thirty-five, he did his first work of consequence on his own, the church of San Carlo alle Quattro Fontane. He began work on Sant'Ivo alla Sapienza in 1642.

Just below us, at the end of Giacomo della Porta's courtyard in the Palazzo alla Sapienza stands one of Rome's most clever architectural surprises. Borromini received the commission to do the work for Sant'Ivo alla Sapienza from Pope Urban VIII. Pope Urban VIII was of the Barberini family, whose family symbol was the bee. It is said that the unique plan for the building was inspired by this symbol. The plan is derived from two intersecting equilateral triangles that form a six-pointed star on the outside and a perfect hexagon on the inside (a hexagram). With the addition of segments of a circle to the design, a stylized bee emerges. The bee is the symbol for charity and prudence; the triangle represents the Trinity; and the star represents wisdom, or *sapienza*. Borromini was always seeking new possibilities for renewing the language of architecture. He used geometry as the means to control space, and by using concave and convex forms he broke away from the static quality of the flat wall. This new spatial language is demonstrated clearly and simply in the interior of this church. The dome that soars upward is about dynamic space. It is light, airy, and is perhaps one of the most original works of architecture in history.

Today the church is difficult to visit, since it is only open Sunday mornings for ten o'clock mass. The interior is bare and is like a large whitewashed lecture hall. It is pure space and has none of the Baroque decoration to distract you. In this amazing space we are reminded of Borromini's proud words, "I would not have joined this profession with the aim of being merely an imitator."

Returning to the Corso we come to the huge building of the Collegio Romano (Jesuit School) standing on the Piazza del Collegio Romano. On the Piazza del Collegio Romano we also find the entrance to the Palazzo-Galleria Doria Pamphili, a vast building whose main facade is on the Corso. This is one of Rome's largest palaces, with more than one thousand rooms, five courtyards, three entrances, four monumental staircases, and a large internal loggia. Part of this giant labyrinth is open to the public and contains the art collection of the Galleria Doria Pamphili. The four galleries exhibit many fine works of art, including work from Titian, Caravaggio, Raphael, Brueghel, Bernini, Velazquez, and Claude Lorrain.

If you would like to see what it was like to live in one of these splendid palazzi, take the thirty-minute guided tour. On the tour you will see a portion of the private apartments: the ballroom, the chapel, the winter garden, and the Andrea Doria Room, which is dedicated to the legendary sixteenth-century admiral.

We turn from the Corso onto the smallest of streets, the Vicolo Doria, which runs next to the palace, then turns onto the Via del Plebiscito. The naming of this single small street reflects the changing life in Rome. Until 1871 the Vicolo Doria was called Via della Stufa after one of the city's public baths that once stood near here. In the 1930s, after Mussolini declared war on Ethiopia, the League of Nations applied economic sanctions to Italy. To augment the dwindling gold reserve, Mussolini organized a "voluntary" collection of all gold wedding rings. Not only did the Princess Doria, a Scotswoman, refuse to surrender her ring, but the prince, who was an anti-Fascist, refused to fly a flag from his palace to celebrate the collection. Consequently the palace was broken into by demonstrating Fascists and the family name was removed from the adjoining street and replaced with Vicolo della Fede. *Fede* in Italian means both "faith" and "wedding ring." After the fall of Mussolini, the name of the street quietly returned to Vicolo Doria.

Between the Corso and the Vicolo Doria is the Palazzo Bonaparte. This was the last place that Napoleon's mother lived after Waterloo. She died here in 1836.

Here the Corso opens up onto Piazza Venezia. To our right, facing the Via del Plebiscito, we can see that the ground floor of the Palazzo Doria is lined with shops along the street. Even though these palaces were the homes of the princes of the Holy Roman Empire, the ground floors usually contained shops that opened out onto the street. This practice is most likely a tradition handed down from classical Rome when the *insulae*, the "apartment blocks," were built in a similar manner. Like the *insulae* the palaces, which were built for one owner, are divided up into many separate apartments. The grandest apartment was located on the first floor above the ground, the *piano nobile*. This was the apartment that belonged to the most important members of the family. The rest of the palace would be allocated to other family members and dependents—both gentlemen and ladies-in-waiting, artists, musicians, and servants or other hangers-on. Stories abound how in the gardens of these magnificent palaces pigs or chickens would be kept by some of the more cantankerous relatives. A Roman prince had under one roof the colorful members of his family and those who were there to wait on him. This place, his palace, was his own world.

Piazza Venezia   We are now in the Piazza Venezia. This is the space into which the Corso empties, the present city's modern traffic hub. To the east stands the Palazzo Venezia. Built in 1455 it is the first great Renaissance palace in Rome, and, until the building of the Palazzo del Quirinale in the sixteenth century, Palazzo Venezia was the official residence of the popes. With its tower and machicolations, the moody palace recalls its original purpose as a medieval fortress for a Roman prince who once waged war in the city. The Palazzo Venezia houses the Museo di Palazzo Venezia, with its collection of medieval and Renaissance weapons, and arts and crafts objects. Within the walls of this vast palazzo is a courtyard that is surrounded by Leon Battista Alberti's double-height loggia. One of the city's largest courtyards containing shade trees, fountains, and palm trees, this tranquil oasis is also open to the public.

The Monumento Vittorio Emanuele, the "Vittoriano," was built to commemorate Victor Emmanuel II, the "Father of the Nation." Since we began our walk, the giant columns of the Vittoriano's enormous loggia have filled our vision, and now it is before us. This monument, the great white marble mountain, is grandiose and yet is full of hope. This was to be the best of the best. In 1878 an international competition was held to find the best design. Two hundred and ninety-nine competitors submitted projects. No award was given because of the controversy surrounding the final decision of the design jury. Then a second competition was held, and in 1884 the first prize was awarded to Giuseppe Sacconi. Construction began the following year and, after enormous difficulty, was completed in 1911. After the slaughter of World War I, the Altar to the Nation and the Tomb of the Unknown Soldier were added to the monument.

The Vittoriano is not a favorite of the Romans, yet almost all who visit the city are attracted to it. It has been called everything from a set of false teeth to a wedding cake. There is an equestrian statue of Victor Emmanuel II in the center. Two colossal bronze chariots, driven by winged victories, are on the propylaea. The monument is white *botticino* marble. It is gleaming. The monument has a magnetic effect on those who visit and photograph it from all angles.

Besides its role as one of the city's landmarks, this massive marble

Palazzo Venezia

Piazza Venezia

mountain houses the Istituto per la Storia del Risorgimento, where an entire torpedo boat is on display. In the collection we can also find several objects that belonged to both Giuseppe Mazzini and Giuseppe Garibaldi.

Before we leave Piazza Venezia, probably the least Roman of all the city's squares and one that was nearly destroyed over the past 120 years by town planners' urban-renewal projects, we can still see some of what used to be here. On each side of the Vittoriano are small fragments from Rome's past. To the right are the remains of an *insula* from the first century. To the left of the monument we can see a fragment of a stone wall and a doorway. This is all that remains of the Tomb of Caius Publius Bibulus, erected in the first century B.C. History tells us that the tomb stood at the beginning of the ancient Via Flaminia, now the Corso. The tomb has been a landmark ever since. Petrarch (1304–74) tells us that he wrote one of his sonnets while leaning against it; and it was here, beginning in 1466, that the riderless horses, from the race that ended eight days of the Carnival, were captured in a great white sheet stretched across the street. In 1870, before the expansion of the piazza began, a walled garden stood next to the Palazzo Venezia and was connected to the tower. This, too, was removed to make way for the monument.

Across Piazza Venezia is a twentieth-century "Renaissance" palace. In 1911, the original, along with Michelangelo's house, was demolished to improve the view to the Monumento Vittorio Emanuele.

It was the builder of the Palazzo Venezia and its garden, Pope Paul II, who expanded the Carnival and moved it from the Capitol. In order for him to watch the celebration from his newly built palace, he ordered the Carnival to be held in the Via Lata. During the Carnival the *corse* (races) were run through the streets. Over time the name of the main street of the city changed to Via del Corso. In the cool of the evening the Corso is still the place of races, only now a mere sheet stretched across the street will not stop the Alfas and Fiats as they fly around the open piazza.

The Campidoglio   This morning we are up and on our way by eight to continue our walk. We stop at one of our favorite bars and have a brioche and a cappuccino on the run — the typical Italian breakfast. If you want to see the real Rome, all you have to do is get out early. It is generally too early for all but the most serious tourists, leaving the streets to the shop-keepers and the thousands of office workers on their way to the scores of banks and government buildings located throughout the city center.

After navigating the Piazza Venezia again, we arrive at the *cordonata* (gentle ramped staircase) that leads up to the Piazza del Campidoglio. The Campidoglio, or Capitol, is the smallest of Rome's original seven hills but is probably the most famous. It was the seat of power, the religious center, and for many centuries the head of the civilized world. This is the place where Petrarch received the poet's laurel crown, where Montaigne became one with the temples that once stood there, and the place where in 1764 Gibbon was inspired to write the now-famous *History of the Decline and Fall of the Roman Empire*. This is the place whose name, the Capitol, was given to the seats of government of the new nations that were to come into being in the centuries to follow.

The Capitol, more than any other place in Rome, provides the link between the ancient world and the modern world. The Capitol is still the home to the Roman city government, whose immortal S.P.Q.R. — Senatus Populusque Romanus — is found on everything from drain covers to buses. These initials serve as everyday reminders of Rome's extraordinary relationship to the past.

Along the northern ridge little survives of the ancient fortress with the temple of Juno Moneta, which was near the site of the original *moneta*, or mint. Except for what remains for the archaeologist to find, little exists of the ancient Capitol — the temple of Jupiter Optimus Maximus Capitolinus — which once ran along the southern ridge. Today most of what we see of the Capitol centers on the piazza designed by Michelangelo for Emperor Charles V's ceremonial entry into Rome in 1536. Pope Paul III asked Michelangelo to design the place of arrival for the Holy Roman Emperor's triumphal procession marking his victory over the infidel in North Africa. The brilliance of the design is only fully understood when

Campidoglio

we know the task set before Michelangelo. The Palazzo Senatorio—which was built over the ruins of the ancient Tabularium in 1144—and, to its right, the fifteenth-century Palazzo dei Conservatori already existed on the site and were to be preserved. The most famous equestrian bronze statue, that of Marcus Aurelius, was to be placed in the center of the piazza. And finally, there was very little space to meet the Pope's expectations for Charles V's victorious entry into Rome.

By the placement of another palace, the Palazzo Nuovo, opposite and symmetrical to the Palazzo dei Conservatori, the piazza was given a trapezoidal shape. With the Palazzo Senatorio centered on the long end of the piazza facing the entrance at the shorter end, Michelangelo achieved a sense that the space is opening out as one arrives at the top of the hill. To further enhance the trapezoidal space, the now-famous oval paving design was centered in the piazza. By depressing the oval by a few steps, then gradually raising the center of the oval to the pedestal of the statue, Michelangelo gave the statue the position of honor.

The Museo Capitolino, which is in the Palazzo Nuovo, and the Museo del Palazzo dei Conservatori contain an ancient collection of Classical art originally organized for Pope Sixtus IV and further enriched by later popes. Upstairs in the Palazzo dei Conservatori are my two favorites in this collection: the first century B.C. Greek bronze *Boy with the Thorn* and the lightning-damaged *Capitoline Wolf*, an Etruscan bronze from the sixth century B.C. Installed in one wing of the Palazzo dei Conservatori is the Pinacoteca Capitolina, a picture gallery founded in the eighteenth century by Pope Benedict XIV. It contains work from many painters, including Titian and Caravaggio.

After spending some time viewing the collection we return to the piazza and descend the gentle ramp, but before we leave we must visit the Santa Maria d'Aracoeli. Compared to the *cordonata* of the Campidoglio, the one hundred and twenty-two steps of the Aracoeli—which appear to go straight up—seem daunting. If the *cordonata* represents the ideals of Renaissance life, then the stairs of the Aracoeli suggest the medieval concept of life as a weary pilgrimage leading eventually to heaven. This is completely understandable. The stairs leading to the Aracoeli were built as a

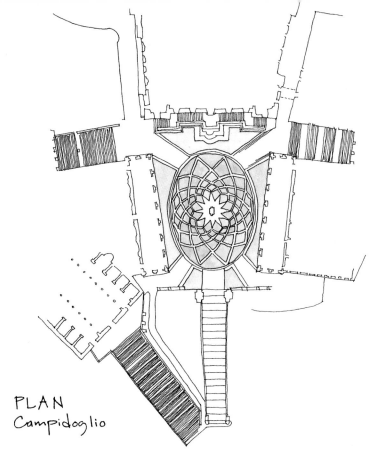

PLAN
Campidoglio

thanksgiving for Rome's delivery from the Black Death in 1348. And, yes, the climb is worth it. The church is perhaps the most Roman of all Roman churches. Built on the ruins of a pagan temple, now consecrated to the Madonna, this is a transformation that is typical in Italy. As we walk around the church, it is as if we are turning the pages of Rome's history. Magnificent columns that once belonged to the classical temples and palaces now hold up a spectacular gilded ceiling commemorating the victory at Lepanto, which ended Turkish dominance of the Mediterranean. The Cosmati pavement is checkered with the tombstones of the famous men who lived and worked in Rome over the centuries. And in the last chapel, near the door, is the most famous *presepio* (Christmas crib) in Rome, where from Christmas Eve to Epiphany, the *Santo Bambino*—the figure of the Holy Child believed to work miracles—stands covered in jewels.

■   ■   ■

Campidoglio

This evening, after a long leisurely dinner, we remember the day's visit to the Capitol and return to the hill where most of the day was spent. The city is quiet. The hill is quiet. The night air is cooled by the *pontentino* (little wind from the sea), which brings with it the fresh scent of cypress and oleander. When seen in the moonlight on a clear summer night, the view from the Capitol to the Forum is an unforgettable sight. With the Forum below and the Colosseum filling the horizon beyond, we are looking at one of the most beautiful sights anywhere, and it is found only in Rome.

By day one requires the knowledge of an archaeologist to understand what must have existed. By night all that is needed is the imagination of the poet to conjure up what must have been. It is almost possible to see the faint glow of the sacred fire silhouetting the marble columns of the Temple of Vesta. Returning to Piazza Venezia, we find that the darkness has enhanced the theatrical quality of the Classical statues. The giant figures of Castor and Pollux, which guard the top of the *cordonata,* appear as actors in some ancient drama.

Via di Ripetta

This morning we are off to explore the last of the three streets that radiate from the Piazza del Popolo, the Via di Ripetta. This is a fairly quiet street until we get to Piazza Augusto Imperatore, with the massive ruins of the Mausoleo di Augusto (Mausoleum of Augustus). The Mausoleum stands in the middle of the piazza, protected by an eight-foot-high chain-link fence. In the morning, with traffic speeding by, it is difficult to imagine that we are standing at the edge of the famous Campus Martius. Located between the Roman Forum and the Tiber River, Campus Martius (Field of Mars) reached its zenith during the Augustan period when the Theater of Marcellus, the Pantheon, the Ara Pacis, and the magnificent Mausoleum of Augustus were erected. Only the tomb now stands to remind us of the immortal Field of Mars. Named after Mars, the Roman god of war, this was the center for Rome's military. The Mausoleum of Augustus, originally built for Augustus and his family and said to have been inspired by the Mausoleum of Alexander the Great in Alexandria, was more than 144 feet high and planted with rows of cypress trees. This monument barely retains the same dignity as we see in the Castel Sant'Angelo (Hadrian's tomb), which stands across the river. The Mausoleum of Augustus has suffered greatly during its lifetime. In the twelfth century it was a fortress. Later it became a vineyard and then a Renaissance garden. In the eighteenth century it became a bullring, then a concert hall. Finally it was to be the tomb of Mussolini. Today we find the great tomb of Augustus a place where garbage is dumped. What was once a great monument is now home to Rome's wild cats and is surrounded by austere modern buildings.

In one of these austere modern glass buildings we find the Ara Pacis Augustae (Altar of Augustan Peace), protected from the elements and visible for all to see day or night. This altar is dedicated to the hard-won peace after victories in Gaul and Spain and also praises an emperor, Augustus, who would later be declared divine. The Altar of Augustan Peace is one of the most remarkable archaeological projects of our time. In 1903 the first scientific excavations took place and revealed the altar *in situ* (in place) in the Campus Martius. To prevent the excavations from flooding, the source of the water and the surrounding area were frozen to a depth of nearly thirty-three feet. The various fragments of the altar, which had been on exhibit in museums around the world, were returned, and the pieces that were still lost were reproduced. The altar was then moved to its present location and reassembled. It finally became completely restored in 1938.

As we leave the Piazza Augusto Imperatore, off to the east we see the dome of San Carlo al Corso cascade down into the piazza, providing us quite a dramatic contrast to the crumbling mausoleum.

Wedged between the Via di Ripetta and the piazza stands San Rocco. This early sixteenth-century church began as a little chapel for the brotherhood of innkeepers and bargemen of the Porto di Ripetta. Prior to the excavation of the Mausoleum of Augustus, the hospital known as *Cellata*, or the Closet, stood just beside the church. This small hospital was used by unmarried expectant mothers, who were not required to give their names. No outside authorities had jurisdiction, nor were they allowed to enter the premises. The hospital is no longer here—it's only a memory that speaks loudly about the shelter it must have offered to those in need.

Connected to San Rocco by an arch is the fifteenth-century Illyrian church San Girolamo degli Schiavoni. The Illyrians founded this church in 1441 after they fled their country in the face of the Turkish advance. The facade of this church was designed to face the Porto di Ripetta. This port on the Tiber River was one of Rome's finest works of Baroque architecture.

In the nineteenth century a series of quays, based on the Parisian model, were built to regulate the flow of the Tiber. This was one of the most unfortunate incidences of the nineteenth century because it called for the destruction of the Porto di Ripetta. The port greatly influenced Francesco de Sanctis' design of the Spanish Steps. For those arriving by water the port was their main entrance to the city. The oval piazza of the main port was centered on the church of San Girolamo degli Schiavoni. A striking double flight of ingeniously curved steps wrapped around a central lookout and led to the water's edge. This was the place of barges and seamen; a place of work. All of this activity made Porto di Ripetta one of the most wonderful ways to arrive to the city.

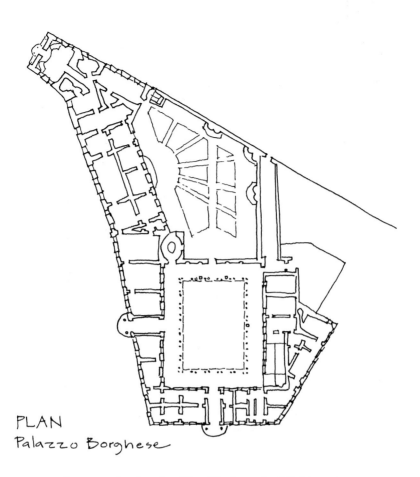

PLAN
Palazzo Borghese

Just past the church of San Girolamo degli Schiavoni we come to "il cembalo" (the harpsichord). The Palazzo Borghese, the most splendid palace in the entire area, gets this unusual name from the unique and irregular plan of the palace. In 1612 Cardinal Scipione Borghese began the construction of a beautiful loggia at the small end of the "harpsichord," which opens up to a fine view of the river. Flaminio Ponzio's main facade, which faces the Piazza Borghese, is well balanced and plainer with a double-story entranceway and is built in the same dignified tradition as that of the Palazzo Farnese. Although the palace still belongs to the Borghese family, the courtyard is open to the public by way of the entrance on Largo Fontanella di Borghese. By allowing us to visit this magnificent courtyard, the Borghese family has given us a wonderful gift. The great court is defined

Palazzo Borghese

by ninety-six Doric and Ionic columns, which are arranged in pairs to support double loggias. Veiled behind the arcade is Rainaldi's superb garden, one of the most complete and best preserved Baroque gardens in Rome. In the heart of Rome's urban environment, this splendid garden with its lily pond provides the palace with a private "ideal" landscape. In this setting, it is easy to imagine the pageantry of the seventeenth-century life that once belonged to this great palace: the arrival of great gilded coaches carrying beautiful ladies and their gentlemen or the arrival of an important cardinal with his cohort of guards. Or one might even have glimpsed the racy Paolina Bonaparte Borghese, Napoleon's favorite sister, whom Canova immortalized in his famous statue of her. To understand how grand the interior of the palace must have been, we need only to visit the Galleria

Borghese in the Villa Borghese to see Cardinal Scipione Borghese's fantastic art collection, which was once kept here.

Piazza Borghese has another special treat, the famous print market. There is something to be found here at every price and for all tastes. I once found the title page of a book on Palladian drawings signed "R. Adams, Architect" (the eighteenth-century British architect) for sale here. The surrounding area of Piazza Borghese is home to hundreds of small antique shops and artisans offering a staggering selection of "objets d'art." In October the famous artisans' fair is held on the Via dell'Orso.

As we continue our walk along the Via della Scrofa (the extension of Via di Ripetta), we find ourselves in a prosperous middle-class district of the late fifteenth century—a rare find in Rome. This area was the result of the cautious town planning policy of Sixtus IV. The streets are narrow and are packed with small houses and shops. The houses are humble and yet possess an architectural dignity that reflects the spirit of their time. The townscape here is intimate, human, and rich with variety—one of my favorite townscapes in the city.

The street where the *coppelle* (small barrels) were made, the Via delle Coppelle, is to our left and leads to the Piazza di Campo Marzio. The piazza is a small, irregular space where you will find an ancient altar and Ionic columns from a forgotten Classical building embedded into the walls of two of the shops. Via della Scrofa veers off to our left and disappears behind a wall of buildings. And Via di Sant'Agostino is to our right. We are now in the heart of the old medieval quarter; the heart of the Campus Martius.

Just to our right is the Piazza di Sant'Agostino, which is always in shadow. Squeezed into this little square, rising out of the piazza and gleaming white in the midday sun is one of Rome's earliest Renaissance churches, Sant'Agostino, built around 1480. The facade with its two side scrolls was constructed from travertine plundered from the Colosseum. The church was designed using the new architectural concepts of the day, showing the influence of Leon Battista Alberti, who designed the facade of Santa Maria Novella in Florence.

Like many Roman churches, Sant'Agostino has an intriguing history. In the eighteenth century the church was the center for the Roman humanists. Henry Alford, the nineteenth-century scholar who was the Dean of Canterbury, described the church as "the Methodist meeting-house of Rome, where the extravagance of the enthusiasm of the lower orders is allowed freest scope." Here is where Cesare Borgia's mistress, the beautiful Fiammetta, had her own chapel and where other famous members of her profession were buried. All memories of these women have disappeared from the interior of Sant'Agostino.

In the mid-eighteenth century the interior was completely and extravagantly refurbished. A Byzantine Madonna brought from Constantinople looks upon Bernini's high altar. The *Madonna di Loreto*, by Caravaggio, is in the first chapel on the left. Down the left aisle, painted on the third column, is Raphael's famous *Prophet Isaiah*, and on the right near the entrance is Jacopo Sansovino's *Madonna del Parto*, or *Madonna of the Childbirth*. The "polished" left foot testifies that this statue is revered by pregnant women, who touch this foot of the statue seeking a safe labor.

Sitting outside on the steps that roll down into the little piazza, and reflecting on the many works of art inside, we turn our discussion to Raphael's *Prophet Isaiah*, painted in 1512. We all agree that it would be one of the great experiences of our lives to have been present when John Goritz (who commissioned the painting) complained to Michelangelo that he had paid too much, and Michelangelo simply said, "The knee alone is worth the price."

In the early part of the sixteenth century Raphael emerged as the leading artist of the city. He controlled a vast network of craftsmen and was involved in a large range of projects—from redesigning the city to designing and constructing buildings, to painting, and to supervising the rescue of ancient work. He even produced a series of theatrical productions. This approach to working in many areas simultaneously ultimately emerged as a coherent and easily recognizable modern style—the Renaissance style. In 1520, at the age of thirty-seven, Raphael died.

Rome is a city of archways. The only way to continue our journey from the Piazza di Sant'Agostino is to walk through an arch, wide enough to drive a small truck through, that pierces a massive wall. Passing through the arch we find the Piazza della Cinque Lune, which is now a chaotic parking lot. Leading away from this piazza are two wide, straight streets. One is the Corso del Rinascimento, which runs past the Palazzo Madama and terminates at the gleaming white facade of Sant'Andrea della Valle. The other is the Via dei Coronari, whose entire length is lined predominately with antique shops. Across the Piazza della Cinque Lune we see what seems to be Rome's smallest archway, the Passetto della Cinque Lune. As soon as we enter this archway, we can see the Piazza Navona, the ancient Circus Agonalis, stretching before us.

Figure-ground showing
Piazza Navona and
the surrounding area

1.

Piazza di Sant' Agostino

2.
Sant' Agostino

3.
Piazza della Cinque Lune

4.

Passetto della Cinque Lune

5.

Passetto della
Cinque Lune

6.
Piazza Navona

Piazza Navona   The Piazza Navona to this day preserves the exact outline of Domitian's (A.D. 81–96) stadium. If you take the little Via del Circo Agonale—on the east side of the piazza—you can see the ruins of Domitian's stadium. Originally the piazza was the place of athletic games. Over the years it has been used for medieval jousting, horse races, and water festivals. During the water festivals that were reminiscent of the ancient *naumachia* (mock sea battles) once held nearby, the entire piazza was flooded.

Piazza Navona is like a Baroque stage set. At the south end is one of two Bernini fountains, the Fountain of the Moor. His other fountain, the famous Fountain of the Four Rivers, dominates the center of the square. Bernini personally carved the horse that represents the Danube River. From these fountains flowed water from the Acqua Vergine—the best water in Rome. Two major architectural works are found along the square: the Palazzo Pamphili (now the Brazilian embassy) and Borromini's church of Sant'Agnese in Agone. Sant'Agnese in Agone was built on the exact spot

Piazza Navona

where the beautiful thirteen-year-old saint began her martyrdom by being stripped in a Roman brothel before a jeering crowd. Just as she was to be paraded naked into the piazza, her hair grew to a miraculous length concealing her nakedness. Together with the mellow ochre houses that ring the square, Piazza Navona is the most picturesque in Rome. Only the month-long celebration of the Epiphany Fair in December keeps the festive spirit of the old square alive.

The old market that once flourished here is now gone, and the piazza is no longer flooded for the water festival, but it is still a favorite of tourists and locals alike. It is perhaps the most lively place in all of Rome. Artists of all ranges sell their work by day under the shade of an umbrella and by night under the glow of propane lights. Some will paint as you watch; others will paint your portrait for a small price. I prefer to sip coffee at Columbia's or have an ice cream at Tre Scalini's and watch the world go by.

After coffee and some time spent drawing, it is time to visit one of the most intriguing churches in the city. By taking the Via Sant'Agnese, alongside Sant'Agnese in Agone, and then continuing to Via di Tor Millina, within a minute we reach Via di Parione. Tucked away at the end of this dark street is Pietro da Cortona's Baroque masterpiece, the Santa Maria della Pace. The little church has a splendid convex facade, preceded by a semicircular porch that extends into the middle of the piazza. Besides designing the new facade, Cortona also redesigned and enlarged the open area in front of the church, creating a beautiful little piazza

Santa Maria della Pace

that wraps around the porch, inviting us to enter and welcoming us to the church.

Just to our right as we enter are the *Sibyls*, the famous frescoes by Raphael. If the *Sibyls* are the jewel inside, then the cloister is the jewel outside. Alongside the church stands the cloister. Donato Bramante's first commission in Rome was designed after five years of studying and measuring the ruins of antiquity. On warm summer evenings the small cloister with its elegant double arcade is the venue for open-air recitals. Tonight it is Chopin, a suitable selection to reflect the classic dignity of this serene place. After the recital the popular Bar della Pace, just in front of the church, is the perfect place to gather for a drink or a light meal and enjoy the warmth of the Roman night.

Via della Pace

At the south end of Piazza Navona is the Via della Posta Vecchia, a winding little street that leads to the Piazza dei Massimi with its curious freestanding column. This little street then leads onto Piazza Sant'Andrea della Valle, which is off the Corso Vittorio Emanuele II. Following the curve of the street is the main facade of the Palazzo Massimo alle Colonne, Baldassare Peruzzi's masterpiece. The main architectural feature of the palazzo is the six squat Doric columns that frame the portico on the main facade. In the courtyard, Peruzzi opened up the walls above the columns to give the courtyard a feeling of openness and lightness.

We are now on the Corso Vittorio Emanuele II, in the area known as the *valle* (valley). In classical times the low-lying marsh was excavated by Agrippa to form an artificial lake, the Stagnum Agrippae. His famous baths and the surrounding landscape with the quiet lake disappeared long ago, and now cars roar through this once peaceful valley.

In 1881 Italy's new Piedmontese masters built the Corso Vittorio Emanuele II to bring "style and design" to the center of the city. A wide thoroughfare, this street was cut through the tangle of ancient narrow streets to open up a more convenient route to St. Peter's.

Standing across the Corso Vittorio Emanuele II is the church of Sant'Andrea della Valle, one of Rome's largest churches, which took nearly seventy years to complete. Carlo Rainaldi's very tall Baroque travertine facade is punctuated by Ercole Ferrata's lonely Baroque angel. This lonely angel was to have had a companion, but Pope Alexander VII criticized Ercole Ferrata's first angel to the point that the sculptor refused to sculpt the second angel.

Sant'Andrea della Valle's enormous dome by Carlo Maderno is second in size only to that of St. Peter's. Twenty-three-year-old Francesco Borromini assisted Carlo Maderno with the dome's design. The clerestory is Borromini's first work in Rome. This was a humble beginning for the man who would eventually design the twisted lantern of Sant'Ivo.

After crossing the Corso Vittorio Emanuele II in the midday traffic—a truly Roman experience—we reach the splendid Baroque interior of Sant'Andrea della Valle. We are immediately impressed by *The Glory of Paradise*, a vast fresco in the dome by Giovanni Lanfranco. On the pendentives of the dome are Domenichino's monumental figures of the *Evangelists*, which inspired the French author Stendhal to comment in his journal, "There are days when it seems to me painting can go no further." Both Carlo Fontana and Giacomo della Porta have designed chapels here. In the first chapel on the left is a statue by Pietro Bernini, Gian Lorenzo's father. Taken all together, this is truly one of the most exceptional churches and is usually missed by most tourists, except possibly those who recognize the church as the fictional setting for Act 1 of Puccini's *Tosca*.

Just to the west of Sant'Andrea della Valle along the Corso Vittorio Emanuele II we will find the Via Baullari, which leads us to the Piazza Campo dei Fiori.

Piazza Campo dei Fiori   The best time to see the Piazza Campo dei Fiori, or the Field of Flowers, is in the morning when the *campo* is alive with the activities of the busiest fruit, vegetable, and flower markets in Rome. If you arrive early, say by eight, the day's shopping can be quickly completed. The *campo* is a vibrant survivor of old Rome, not necessarily the place for sightseeing, but certainly the place to find the everyday life of Rome. This is the place that is best described as the "living room" for the neighborhood. I remember the first time I went to the *campo*. It was not obvious which direction I had to travel to arrive at my destination. I was lost in the maze of streets. An elderly gentleman, seeing my predicament, offered to escort me personally to the *campo*. After I followed him for a short distance, he presented to me the great open space of his neighborhood as if he were inviting me into his own home. From that moment it was clear to me the importance of these outdoor rooms to the citizens of Rome. This is the place of stallholders, locals, workmen, tramps, and students. Piazza Campo dei Fiori is the place where neighborhood children play among the vendors, chase pigeons, and climb on the grim statue of the monk Giordano Bruno, who was burned at the stake for heresy in 1600. In addition to the *campo*'s being the site of the historic execution of Giordano Bruno, just to the east of the *campo*, buried in the walls of the existing buildings and marked by the pattern of the street, is the Theater of Pompey, in whose great hall Caesar was murdered. Today, shops, cafés, and hotels line the

Campo dei Fiori

Campo dei Fiori

campo. One particular bakery, Forno la Carbonara, on the west end of the *campo,* is famous for its *pizza bianco,* or pizza without tomato sauce.

Next to the bakery the Vicolo del Gallo leads us into the Piazza Farnese, with the Palazzo Farnese on the far side of the piazza. This is one of the finest palaces of the high Renaissance in Rome. To the dismay of many Romans, the palazzo has been the French embassy since 1871. In addition to the imposing main facade, with Michelangelo's cornice, is the atrium, which was designed by Antonio da Sangallo the Younger, with three aisles and quadruple rows of columns leading into the courtyard. It has been said that the harmony and perfect balance of the proportions

of the space were created by using the principles set forth by Vitruvius.

Just a stone's throw from the Palazzo Farnese is the Palazzo Spada with its Galleria, whose facade is decorated with niches filled with figures from antiquity. The palace's famous architectural element, though, is the trompe l'oeil (trick perspective), which leads to the garden gallery. What appears to be a magnificent row of twin columns leading to a large statue is, in reality, only fifty-nine feet long and a small statue. For years it was believed that it was Borromini's genius that was behind this lighthearted design. It is now believed to be the work of an obscure Augustinian priest, Giovanni Mari da Bitonto. Either way, it is still worth a special visit.

No. 28 · 30 · 31 Arco degli Acetari

Via Giulia Behind the Palazzo Farnese is the Via Giulia, probably the most elegant street in old Rome. From where we stand, framed by the great arch that was part of a grand design by Michelangelo to link the Palazzo Farnese with the Villa Farnesina across the river, we can see the whole length of the absolutely straight sixteenth-century street. Bramante himself, Julius II's architect, planned the Via Giulia in 1508 as part of the Pope's complicated scheme for redesigning the road system of the city. After the Pope's adoption of the Vatican as his official seat upon returning from Avi-

Via Giula

gnon, the Via Giulia was one of the first new roads built to help the thousands of pilgrims make their way to St. Peter's, and to prevent them from getting lost in the labyrinth of narrow, medieval streets. In the seventeenth and eighteenth centuries the Via Giulia expanded to the length of more than half a mile. During this time many of Rome's most prestigious architects were responsible for the design of many of the buildings on the Via Giulia. Borromini rebuilt the Palazzo Falconieri adjacent to the arch. Ferdinando Fuga designed the church of Santa Maria dell'Orazione e Morte, and Raphael designed the little church of Sant'Eligio degli Orefici. Today the street is still elegant with its many beautiful buildings lining the way. It is much quieter now; the street's significance in the city is only a memory.

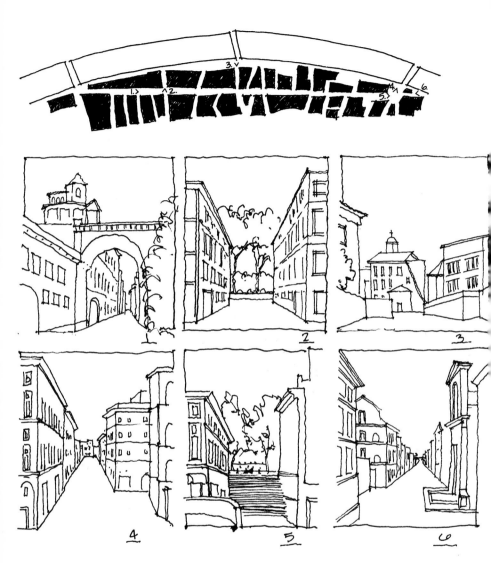

Via Giula

Santa Maria dell' Orazione e Morte

Piazza del Quirinale to Porta Pia

The best approach to Piazza del Quirinale is from the steep steps that lead from the top of the Via della Dataria, only a minute from the Fontana di Trevi. Once we reach the top of the steps we see the large piazza. The piazza is surrounded on three sides by palazzi, with the fourth side open to a panorama of the city that stretches to the dome of St. Peter's and beyond. In the midst of this vast piazza, with cars and scooters swirling around them, stand the famous *Dioscuri*, which are Castor and Pollux, and their steeds. From time immemorial these two colossal statues from the Imperial age have stood on "Monte Cavallo" (Horse Mountain) and have

Piazza del Quirinale

served as one of the important landmarks of the city. The fountain below them was built from a granite basin found near the Temple of the Dioscuri in the Roman Forum. The obelisk that presides over them all is from the Mausoleum of Augustus.

Quirinal Hill is the highest of Rome's seven hills, and its history begins in the Iron Age, around 1300 B.C., when the Sabines settled here. Toward the end of the Imperial age two great baths, those of Diocletian and Constantine, were built on the Quirinal, while the rest of the hill was covered with splendid parks, including the famous park of Sallust. Palazzo del Quirinale began in 1550, when Cardinal Ippolito d'Este rented a villa with a garden on the summit of the Quirinal. The Cardinal enlarged and improved the villa until it became as famous as his villa at Tivoli—Fontana, Maderno, Fuga, and Bernini all contributed to what is now the official residence of the President of the Republic. The graceful entrance on the stern ochre main facade was designed by Bernini and leads to a giant porticoed courtyard with a clock tower rising above the garden, which covers most of the Quirinal Hill. Six-foot or taller cuirassiers of the guard, dressed in crimson and blue uniforms topped with shining chrome helmets with flowing horse tails, protect probably the best cared for garden in all of Rome. A visit to the grounds and the palace, which are generally closed to the public, can be arranged by writing to the Ufficio Intendenza del Quirinale. Once inside you will see the beautiful Cappella Paolina, by Carlo Maderno, the chapel built to the exact shape and dimension as the Sistine Chapel. This is the room where the conclaves were held until 1870. You will also see the *sala degli specchi* (hall of mirrors) with its sparkling Murano glass chandeliers. It would be worth the effort to visit Palazzo del Quirinale just to view Rome's first oval spiral staircase, with paired Tuscan columns, designed by the architect Ottaviano Mascarino in 1585.

As we continue our journey down the Via del Quirinale, we walk past the south edge of the palace, the "long sleeve." This wing, designed by Bernini to accommodate the visiting cardinals, is only two rooms deep but more than thirteen hundred feet long. About halfway down the "sleeve," on our right, we come to a graceful flight of semicircular steps flowing out from under a delicate semicircular porch. We are standing in front of Bernini's most brilliant work, the church of Sant'Andrea al Quirinale. Domenico Bernini, in his biography of his father, Gian Lorenzo, tells us that the architect regarded this as one of his most successful works and that in his old age he sometimes came to sit here and enjoy it.

The unique little church of Sant'Andrea al Quirinale was commissioned in 1658 for the Jesuit novices. The convex walls of the adjacent courtyards frame the confident main facade. Behind the facade we can see the oval cylinder of the central space, with its bold console of buttresses, rise above the surrounding ring of smaller chapels. Once inside we cannot

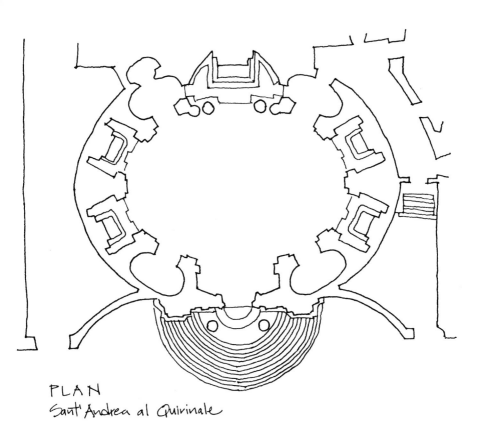

PLAN
Sant' Andrea al Quirinale

help but feel a sense of noble elegance. The elliptical plan is simple: the long axis is parallel to the street; the short axis leads to the altar. The altar is framed by large red *cottanello* marble columns from Sicily. The architecture of the interior is pure and mostly unbroken surfaces of rich-colored marbles. This effect is enhanced by the skillful placement of windows, which allow the dramatic natural light to flow in from above. When we enter the church, our eyes are irresistibly drawn to the life-size statue of St. Andrew, located in a deep niche above the main altar. St. Andrew is gazing toward the heavenly Host, which awaits him in the beautiful gold and white stucco dome.

The church was rarely mentioned in the early guidebooks about Rome, and travelers to the city only occasionally visited the little church. One tourist did visit, the American writer Nathaniel Hawthorne, and

Sant' Andrea al Quirinale

wrote: "I haven't seen, nor expect to see, anything else so entirely and satisfactorily finished as this small oval church—I only wish I could pack it in a large box and send it home."

Just a few steps from Sant'Andrea al Quirinale we discover a small tree-covered garden, a peaceful place to have a picnic lunch and plan the rest of the day's schedule. As we enjoy our lunch of fresh bread, *pecorino*—a sharp cheese—and oranges, we are still in quiet awe of Bernini's little Baroque church. Its careful attention to design. Its attention to detail. We quickly begin to admire those who worked on it carefully and skillfully. It is easy to see why it took twelve years to complete.

Just beyond the garden is the intersection of two roads opened by Pope Sixtus V during his great urban reforms of the sixteenth century. We are on the corner of the Via del Quirinale and the Via delle Quattro Fontane. At this corner, more than any other, the meaning of Sixtus V's city plan is confirmed. To ensure that his plans would be carried forward, and that the appropriate development would happen at this intersection, Pope Sixtus V commissioned four fountains to be built, one for each corner. Each fountain has a statue of either the Tiber, the Nile, the goddess Diana, or the goddess Juno. This is the famous "Quadrivio delle Quattro Fontane" (Crossroads of the Four Fountains).

From this intersection we can see four monuments. To the south, we see the obelisk of Santa Maria Maggiore standing on top of the Esquiline Hill. Straight ahead, to the east, we see Michelangelo's Porta Pia. To the north, we see the obelisk that stands in front of the Trinità dei Monti, and behind us, the fourth monument, an obelisk in the Piazza del Quirinale.

On the Quadrivio delle Quattro Fontane stands Borromini's first commission. In 1634, after spending twenty years as a stonecutter and a draftsman, he was asked by the Spanish order of the Discalced Trinitarians to build the church and monastery of San Carlo alle Quattro Fontane. On the narrow corner site Borromini began building the dormitory, refectory, and the cloisters. By 1638 the body of the church was completed and the funding was exhausted. In 1665, after a delay of twenty-seven years, Borromini resumed work on the facade. He had completed only the first order

San Carlo alle Quattro Fontane

when he died in 1667, making San Carlo alle Quattro Fontane his first commission and last. The swirling concave-convex facade was completed by his nephew Bernardo. The square bell tower is entirely Bernardo's work, and it replaced the original triangular bell tower that was begun by Borromini.

Whereas most of the work on the exterior was completed by Bernardo, the interior is the work of Borromini. During this time, when most of the architecture was based on the proportions of the human body, Borromini was primarily concerned with an architecture that was based on geometric form. As a result much of his work appears eccentric and bizarre, appealing to one's heart and soul. The plan of the church is based on equilateral triangles and circles, resulting in a plan that is roughly in the shape of a diamond, with rounded ends and curved diagonals.

The movement created by the walls is what first grabs our attention. The walls, together with the columns, have been treated in a sculptural manner. Except for the few touches of gilding in the altarpiece, the interior of the church is plain white stucco, revealing clearly the form of the structure and allowing for an uninterrupted flow of space. In this interior the statues are part of the architecture and are not freestanding, as was the common practice of the day. The most remarkable aspect of this strangely shaped space is the oval dome that is suspended over it. This extraordinary effect is achieved by the light that enters from partially concealed windows lining the base of the dome. I can only wonder

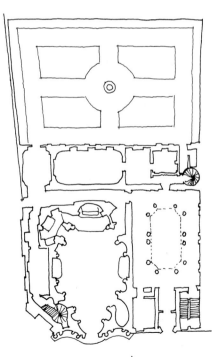

PLAN San Carlino

if this was the inspiration for the domes of the Palazzetto and Palazzo dello Sport designed by Pier Luigi Nervi for the 1960 Olympic Games.

The cloister is carefully placed alongside the church. The corners of the small rectangular space have been replaced with curved sections, reminding us of the curious shape of the interior of the church. With Borromini what is most interesting is his attention to every detail. Without large surfaces to work with, Borromini turned to the balusters to create a special effect of movement. Instead of traditional balusters with circular bases, he created a baluster with a triangular base that curves slightly inward on each side. The balusters were arranged so that they alternate between having the thickest section of the baluster at the top to having the thickest section of the baluster at the bottom. What appeared to be an insignificant detail created an extraordinary sense of movement, the hallmark of Baroque architecture.

Almost immediately after its completion, this little church, San Carlo alle Quattro Fontane (which the locals call "San Carlino") began receiving requests from around the world for copies of the architectural plans. They too wanted their very own San Carlino. The highest praise for Borromini's first original work came from the Procurator General of the Spanish Order when he wrote, "In the opinion of everybody, nothing similar as regards artistic merit, originality, excellence and singularity can be found anywhere in the world. Everything is ordered so that each part completes the next, and the spectator is invited to let his eyes run ceaselessly over the structure."

San Carlino and Sant'Andrea al Quirinale stand almost next to each other. Within half an hour we can study two of the most important works by two of the great architectural rivals of seventeenth-century Rome. Bernini, the traditionalist, was the son of a successful father. Bernini's life contrasted sharply with that of Borromini, who worked his way up through the ranks and was the innovator who challenged the accepted concepts of architecture. This rivalry was so intense that it ultimately drove Borromini to suicide. Via del Quirinale, with its two wonderful churches, will always be, to me, the street of the dueling churches.

As we continue our walk east along the Via XX Settembre we pass the massive Ministero del Bilancio e Tesoro, a building twice the size of the Colosseum. We walk until we finally reach Michelangelo's Porta Pia (Gate of Pius), which is facing into the full sunlight of early evening. The Porta Pia rises up and reminds me of one of Serlio's stage sets showing a broad straight street in perspective ending in a monumental arch. Commissioned in 1561, after the Romans had abandoned hope of using the ancient Aurelian Walls as a defense against modern artillery, the gate was designed to celebrate the arrival of princes. The Porta Pia faces inward toward the city and goes against the tradition that from ancient times positioned the gate toward the road and the open countryside. Michelangelo's gate has more to do with the street than the wall. It is about urban

Porta Pia

townscape; it was designed to end the street. The Via XX Settembre visually terminates at the imposing facade of the gate at this end and at the colossal statues of the *Dioscuri* at the other end. This is where Pope Sixtus V ensured that a visual connection would be made between the two monuments by lowering the grade of the street as much as four feet.

Just as Michelangelo exercised control over the whole of the hill at the Capitol, his gateway does the same to the street. By now we know that the Sistine plan is characterized by long street vistas that are terminated by obelisks. The obelisk gives the pedestrian a measure of distance, a goal that rises above the buildings and becomes part of the skyline. The narrow attic of the gate, where Pius IV also wanted to place an obelisk, serves in much the same manner. The portal and the attic are central to the design and are intended to be seen from a distance.

I think the most interesting aspect of the Porta Pia is the central portal. From drawings made by Michelangelo we know that this was his primary preoccupation for the design of the gate. He searched intuitively and ultimately found fantastic combinations: hard-edge forms against soft, deep shadows next to light, and, in the main opening, the broken square arch is located under a round relieving arch. The portal has the most complex detail and variety of curves and angles of the time. Professor Rasmussen, the noted architectural historian, believes that Michelangelo's design of the gate "is deliberately restless, . . . to create an architecture that was felt to be dramatic." Although this is Rome's first major Renaissance gate, it is not inspired by either the surviving ancient gates nor the triumphal arches. It recalls the medieval era with its crenellations, which Michelangelo used to support the Medici *palle* (balls).

For many years this gate marked the edge of the city. Beyond the gate stretched the open spaces of the Roman *campagna*, or countryside. All of this changed on September 20, 1870. Rome was a city under siege protected by the French army and the papal mercenaries. The armies of united Italy breached the Aurelian Walls on both sides of the Porta Pia and entered the city. Pius IX surrendered Rome the same day. Miraculously, the Porta Pia was spared, and the name of the street, Via XX Settembre, commemorates the twentieth of September in 1870.

Porta Pia

San Giovanni in Laterano

After a light breakfast we begin our walk at the obelisk on the Spanish Steps in front of the Trinità dei Monti. From here we will work our way south to the church of San Giovanni in Laterano, near the Aurelian Walls.

Setting out on the Via Sistina, we cross the Via del Tritone, one of the busiest shopping streets in Rome. We pass by the Piazza Barberini and Bernini's fountain with the four dolphins, the Fountain of the Triton. Across the piazza is the Palazzo Barberini, a palace by Maderno and Borromini that now houses the Galleria Nazionale d'Arte Antica. Leading up the hill, away from the northeast corner of the piazza, is the tree-lined Via Vittorio Veneto, that infamous street where the rich and famous gathered in *La Dolce Vita*. As we begin to climb the hill of the Via delle Quattro Fontane, we see we have returned to the corner of the four fountains. We can now see the church of Santa Maria Maggiore standing on top of the Esquiline Hill, and the obelisk in the Piazza dell'Esquilino guides us. Moving down the hill, we reach the Via Nazionale, one of the broad streets built in the 1870s. This is one of the city's main shopping streets, particularly good for shoes and women's clothes. At the head of the Via Nazionale is the seedy Piazza della Repubblica. The semicircular perimeter of the piazza traces the giant exedra of the ancient Baths of Diocletian, once the largest in Rome. Inside the enormous remains of the Baths' central *frigidarium* is the Santa Maria degli Angeli. Michelangelo carefully placed the new church within the vast ruins of the Baths, protecting and preserving the existing structure.

On the back side of the Baths is the Museo Nazionale Romano, with the greatest collection of antique sculpture and mosaics in the world. It is just the place to spend long afternoons.

The final leg of the journey is a walk along the Via Depretis. As soon as we cross the Via Cavour we can see the back of the church Santa Maria Maggiore in the midst of parked cars and tour buses. In the Piazza dell'Esquilino stands the second obelisk relocated from the Mausoleum of Augustus. Curiously our journey has taken us to the rear of the church rather than to the front. The axis of the street is aligned with the obelisk.

The twin domes of the church frame the obelisk, thus creating the link back up to Piazza del Popolo. The beautiful exterior of the curved *apse* and the range of stairs were designed by Carlo Rainaldi specifically to formalize this important piece of Roman townscape. On most afternoons you can find boys playing soccer on the stairs, kicking the ball against the curved back of the church.

Slipping around to the front, which faces the Piazza di Santa Maria Maggiore, we see a huge column topped by a statue of the Madonna. This column was brought here from the Basilica of Maxentius, which was the largest basilica in the Forum.

Behind Ferdinando Fuga's facade with its fine loggia, designed in 1743, a treasure house of fine work awaits: ancient columns, fifth-century mosaics, a Renaissance ceiling gilded with what is said to be the first gold from the New World, along with work by Michelangelo, della Porta, and Fontana, are collected here. This basilica is one of Rome's seven churches that have been the chief objects of pilgrimage since time immemorial. Perhaps Sunday we will return here to attend Mass in this great patriarchal basilica.

Standing under the statue of the Madonna in the center of the piazza, I am preparing to risk life and limb to cross through the swarming traffic to reach the Via Merulana—the wide, straight street that leads to the church San Giovanni in Laterano. I am inspired to cross, knowing that we will find lunch. After lunch we plan to visit the Museo Nazionale d'Arte Orientale just down the hill.

The tree-lined Via Merulana provides a fine approach to Piazza di Giovanni in Laterano. In the center of the vast piazza stands the tallest and oldest obelisk in Rome. Dating from the fifteenth century B.C., it was brought from Thebes by Constantine in A.D. 357.

The church San Giovanni in Laterano and the adjoining sober Palazzo del Laterano sit alone on the top of the hill. As we come around to the front of the church we can read the inscription across the facade: MATER ET CAPUT OMNIUM ECCLESIARIUM URBIS ET ORBIS (Mother and head of all the churches of the city and the world). This is Rome's main cathedral. The church has had a long and often troubled history. It was destroyed by

Santa Maria Maggiore

vandals in the fifth century, leveled by an earthquake in the eighth century, all but abandoned when the papacy moved to Avignon, burnt down twice in the fourteenth century, and in the latter part of this century it has been the victim of terrorist bombs. This great church was the scene of Charlemagne's baptism in 774, and the place where the popes were crowned until the nineteenth century.

The main facade, the result of a competition in which twenty-three architects took part, was designed by the relatively unknown architect Alessandro Galilei. Even though the colossal facade was clearly inspired by the facade of St. Peter's, it is the fifteen gigantic statues (Christ, St. John the Baptist, St. John the Evangelist, along with the twelve doctors of the church) that give the facade its character. The fifteen statues are visible from as far away as the Janiculum.

Standing in the portico, I can see a beautiful view over to the Sabine and Alban hills. This view makes the portico a suitable place to find the ancient statue of Constantine. The enormous doors of the central portal are the bronze doors from the original *Curia* (Senate House) of the Roman Forum.

The interior was refurbished in 1650 by Borromini with mixed results. What is impressive is the sheer size of the *nave* and the quality of light it receives. In addition to all the treasures inside, there are two treasures waiting for us outside, the baptistery and the cloister. San Giovanni's baptistery is the only part of the original fourth-century church to have survived. This was the first baptistery in Christendom. Built on the basic octagonal plan, it has since been copied throughout Italy. The small door at the end of the left aisle leads to one of Rome's secrets—hidden within the precinct of the church is the cloister. The cloister represents the high point of the city's Cosmati tradition. Each of the arcade's hundreds of tiny columns are different. Some twisted, some not, and all of them are covered with an intricate mosaic. These magical columns are the work of Jacopo and Pietro Vassalletto (father and son) and were constructed between 1215 and 1223.

Sitting in the portico having completed a long day of exploring the Sistine roads, we can see that the street design of the city has made a difference in our perception of time and distance. Sixtus V's vision was to link the pilgrimage churches and the monuments by a series of roads that would visually appear to shorten the distance between points—and to make the going less strenuous. As Carlo Fontana wrote, "He has built very wide and straight roads so that whether on foot, on horseback or by carriage, one can depart from any point in Rome and reach the famous holy places without difficulty."

San Giovanni in Laterano

Districts

Trastevere

With the help of Rome's efficient bus system we find ourselves on the Via del Portico d'Ottavia before eight in the morning. The street is lined with many interesting shops, including one of the most interesting in Rome, Limentani. For more than one hundred and sixty years every possible type of dish and kitchen utensil has been sold from this enormous store. Inside you will find something in every price range, and in one massive jumble. If this is too overwhelming, then their more modern showroom behind the Portico of Octavia may be more to your liking. Many of the houses on this street date from the early Renaissance, but I think my fascination with the street lies in the huge stumps of Classical columns (relics of the ancient Portico of Octavia) that stick out of the street just ahead.

Nowhere else in Rome are we so aware, so conscious, of the city which is buried beneath us. Originally the portico enclosed the temples dedicated to Juno and Jupiter and served as the meeting place for the adjacent Theater of Marcellus. The famous Medici *Venus* (now in the Uffizi) was discovered in the rubbish of the medieval fish market that once stood here. This was just one of the many statues that resided among the three hundred columns of the portico. Built directly into the ruins is the little church of San Angelo in Pescheria, owing its name to the fish market. To the right of the portico we can still see a plaque embedded in the wall. Legend states that any fish longer than the plaque must have its head and body, up to the first fin, given to the conservators. This section of the fish was considered a delicacy.

Looming up next to us, barely recognizable except for its vast bulk, is the Theater of Marcellus. The once great theater, then medieval fortress, then Renaissance palace, was turned into a maze of apartments during the Fascist era. The upper part of the theater, which is accessible by another street, is still used for summer productions.

The area between the Via del Portico d'Ottavia and the Tiber was called the "Jewish Enclosure" — the Ghetto. This area of barely seven and one-half acres was in constant danger of being flooded and was surrounded by a high wall whose gates were only opened at dawn and then closed at sunset. All Roman Jews were enclosed behind these walls beginning in the middle of the sixteenth century. Six thousand people lived behind those walls. The very people who were acclaimed during the Middle Ages for their abilities were denied the practice of any of their tradi-

tional professions. Much of this began to change when the walls of the Ghetto were demolished in 1848. The dense maze of buildings was demolished in 1885, and in 1888 the rebuilding of the neighborhood began. The synagogue was inaugurated in 1904. Its beautiful dome is considered a symbol of religious equality with the other churches in Rome. Today the Ghetto is one of Rome's most peaceful places, with some of the quietest and most pleasant backstreets.

Rome

San Bartolmeo

Standing in the garden of the synagogue we are offered another one of Rome's stunning vistas. Through the veil of sycamore trees that line the Tiber River, we can see across to the Isola Tiberina, the island in the middle of the Tiber, and beyond into the tattered buildings of Trastevere. Just to the north of the island are the remains of Pons Aemilius, a bridge built around 180 B.C.. In front of us, crossing over to the island, is Rome's oldest surviving bridge, the Ponte Fabricio, built in 62 B.C. by Lucius Fabricius. In contrast to the medieval buildings on the island are the modern bronze statues standing next to the river in the garden of San Bartolomeo. These sleek figures are the work of the locally famous Padre P. A. Martin, one of the two or three Franciscans who still serve San Bartolomeo.

Crossing over to the island we pass the large modern hospital of the Fatebenefratelli. This hospital has the reputation of being the best hospital in Rome if one has an emergency. To our left is the eleventh-century tower of the Pierleoni fortress, the Torre della Contessa. Behind the tower in the corner of the piazza is a small arch leading to the garden along the river. No one seems to be very concerned with the NO ENTRY sign. In the garden, among the statues of Padre Martin, we can still see the old Roman travertine wall built to represent the prow of a ship to commemorate the city's rescue from the plague of 289 B.C. According to legend, during the great plague the Sibylline oracles directed the Romans to visit the famous Greek Temple of Aesculapius. When the ship returned carrying one of the sacred healing snakes, it slid from the boat, swam to the island, and made the island its home. Seeing this as a sign from the gods, a temple was immediately built, later to be rebuilt as San Bartolomeo. For centuries the island has been a place where the sick have been brought in hope of a cure.

At the water's edge the small Piazza di San Bartolomeo invites us to linger and watch the water of the Tiber swirl around the Ponte Cestio. According to an ancient legend, the island formed when the Tarquin family was driven from Rome and dumped all the grain they had harvested from the Campus Martius into the river.

Once across the Ponte Cestio we reach Trastevere (across the Tiber). This is an eccentric neighborhood, a close-knit district where seediness becomes picturesque, where restaurants abound, galleries flourish, and the mellow nightlife lasts till dawn.

When the threat of Etruscan attack ceased in the second century B.C., a new port was opened at the foot of the Aventine Hill across the river. Until then Trastevere had been mostly open meadowland and was not considered part of Rome. From that time forward, even though it was not within the city walls, it became one of the largest and most populated areas of the city. This population was a mixed bag of sailors and immigrants, mostly Syrians and Jews, who made this their home until the Jews were moved across the river into the Ghetto. The inhabitants of Trastevere are a proud people claiming to be the only real Romans to have descended from ancient classical stock. A fiercely independent folk, they boast that a real Trasteverino would never cross the Tiber! In July the people of Trastevere turn out to celebrate the *Festa Noiantri* (Festival of We Others) as a symbol of this independence. They also claim to be the stronghold of Roman dialect poetry, as evidenced by the naming of streets and piazzas after

Trastevere

poets. In fact, just around the corner from here stands a statue of Gioacchino Belli, dressed in a top hat and coat, in the middle of the Piazza Gioacchino Belli.

Much of Rome has been affected by the "commercial miracle" that has brought a variety of trendy shops into the heart of the city. Trastevere is the least affected of all the old *rioni* (neighborhoods) of Rome. The working-class nature of the district has changed very little and retains much of its original character. Trastevere is a web of narrow streets and quiet squares—a delightful place to wander among the scruffy ochre and umber buildings.

Our first stop is the church of Santa Cecilia in Trastevere. Facing the place where the old port of Ripa Grande was once located, it now stands in one of the most unspoilt areas of the district. This is a very old church, probably dating back as far as the fifth century. The most lasting aspect of the church is the Baroque gateway and garden, which are in front of Fuga's facade built in 1741.

The large building along the river, between the churches of Santa Cecilia and San Francesco a Ripa, was the papal poorhouse of San Michele. Bought by the state in 1963, the building is still undergoing restoration. Founded in 1693, San Michele was originally intended to care for orphans and abandoned children. Ultimately all those unwanted by the city found their way here.

We are now at Ponte Sublicio. This is the legendary bridge where the immortal three—Horatius, Herminius, and Spurius Lartius—took their position at the then-wooden bridge to defend Rome against the advancing Etruscans.

At the head of the bridge is Porta Portese, the site of the largest flea market in Europe. On Sunday mornings at dawn the chaos begins. Four thousand stalls open, selling everything from antiques to zucchini. This is the place to arrive early and keep a watchful eye out for pickpockets.

After wandering the narrow streets, stopping for coffee, finding the remains of an eleventh-century synagogue, finding Rome's only English-language movie theater (the shabby but much-loved Pasquino, Vicolo del Piede 19), and generally soaking up the atmosphere of Trastevere, we arrive in the heart and soul of the entire *rione*, Piazza di Santa Maria in Trastevere. In 1972 Fellini filmed scenes for *Roma* in the piazza. Children play soccer here; teenagers hang out at Carlo Maderno's prominent fountain in the middle of the piazza. Tourists and regulars alike linger in any one of the restaurants—especially the expensive Sabatini—that line the square. We have escaped the outside world in this, the main *salon* of Trastevere.

The highlight of the piazza, I think, is not the massive seventeenth-century palace of San Callisto but the exquisite Basilica di Santa Maria in Trastevere. This was the first church in Rome to be dedicated to the Virgin and is quite possibly the oldest official place of Christian worship in the city. A Romanesque campanile towers above Fontana's portico of 1702. But these are not the important features of the facade. What makes this facade special are the glittering gold mosaics above the portico. Had the Baroque church builders not been so ruthless, many similar facades would have survived from the Middle Ages.

Piazza di Santa Maria
in Trastevere

Inside we find more mosaics, and they are even more stunning. The work in the upper *apse* is Byzantine and was probably done by Greek craftsmen about 1100. The work in the lower apse is Pietro Cavallini's, from about 1290. All of this is among a forest of ancient columns that come from the Baths of Caracalla. Underneath it all are swirls of Cosmati pavement in rich tones of red and green marble.

Just around the corner is Piazza Sant'Egidio and the Museum of Folklore and Roman Dialect Poets, and beyond is the Villa Farnesina, with its memorable garden. For now it is time to enjoy a cool drink before our climb to the Janiculum.

The Janiculum Hill

Since the days of the Etruscan invasions, the Janiculum has protected Rome. Today this is the place to take leisurely walks through playgrounds, lush gardens, ancient churches, and patrician villas. Along the southeastern edge of the Janiculum is a wide terrace that offers us one of the most celebrated views of the city: a view across the red-tiled roofs of Trastevere to the tree-covered Palatine and Aventine and beyond to the blue Alban Hills. On this wide terrace stands the church of San Pietro in Montorio.

It was once believed that St. Peter was crucified on this site. A church has stood here since the ninth century. The present church was commissioned in 1481 by Ferdinand and Isabella of Spain. The facade of San Pietro in Montorio is early Renaissance; it is humble yet elegant. As in many churches in Rome, the interior is a miniature museum. The first chapel is believed to be from the designs of Michelangelo. The second chapel seems to glow in the darkened church. This chapel, for the Raimondi family, is one of Bernini's first studies in the use of concealed natural light. The third chapel contains two undisputed masterpieces by Antoniazza Romano: *St. Anne Enthroned* and *Madonna and Child*. The Cappella del Monte, designed by Vasari and the chapel I was most drawn to, contains the tombs of Antonio and Fabiano del Monte, with fine reclining figures sculpted by Bartolomeo Ammanati. The colors of the domed chapel are rich terra-cottas, blue, and white. All is lit from above by a small lantern, and the combination of the color and the light form a space that can only be described as magical. As if this were not enough, this glorious domed chapel in the church on the hill, outside in the courtyard we find Bramante's Tempietto.

Placed snugly within the cloister, the Tempietto stands as if it were some precious reliquary of a most sacred event. This image is exactly what Bramante intended. The Tempietto marks what was the most sacred spot in Rome: the exact place where it was then believed that St. Peter was crucified. The Tempietto is a small circular building with sixteen Doric columns around the *cella* (sanctuary) forming an *ambulacrum* (passage). The interior is simply elegant. The crypt, which is richly decorated, has a large

Tempietto

hole in the center of the floor where, according to legend, stood the cross on which St. Peter was crucified. Though the Tempietto is small, holding only ten people, it is one of the most significant works representing early Renaissance architecture and marks the transition from fifteenth-century ideals to the ideals that followed in the next century.

Across the street from San Pietro in Montorio is a modern temple dedicated to the soldiers Italy lost in the wars of the last century. Following along the Via Garibaldi we find a terrace in front of Fontana Paola that was built with marble taken from the ruins of the Temple of Nerva. On a hot day the fountain is an oasis and provides another of the Janiculum's remarkable panoramas overlooking the city and beyond. Below is the Botanic Garden, where it is possible to find every species of palm as well as sequoias.

Just up the hill is the highest point on the Janiculum, Porta San Pancrazio. This is the famous site where, in 1849, Garibaldi met General Oudinot's French troops, who were threatening the newly formed Roman Republic. In 1848 Giuseppe Mazzini and Giuseppe Garibaldi started the *risorgimento*, or revolution, that eventually led to the unification of Italy in 1870. Every Italian town and village has immortalized these Italian heroes by naming piazzas and streets in their honor.

I take one last view of the city, never tiring of exploring the maze of roofs, television antennae, and private gardens hiding behind heavy Roman walls. Now it is time to leave the Janiculum and work our way back down to Trastevere for lunch.

The Borgo and the Vatican

Since the time of Pope Boniface VIII, the Ponte Sant'Angelo has been the main route to the Vatican. Originally built to link the Mausoleum of Hadrian to the city, this is one of Rome's most distinguished bridges. Once lined with two rows of gallows, the narrow bridge is now lined with the "Breezy Maniacs," Bernini's angels who battle the wind. To the east of the bridge, facing the river, stands the grandiose Palazzo di Giustizia (Palace of Justice), with its winged charioteer high above the main portico. To our left rises the dome of St. Peter's. Across the bridge, right in front of us, are the massive bulwarks of the Castel Sant'Angelo (originally built as the Mausoleum of Hadrian).

Situated on the right bank of the Tiber, where the river curves sharply, is a site with an exceptional panorama. This is where Emperor Hadrian broke the Roman tradition of being entombed in the Mausoleum of Augustus and chose to erect his own sepulchre, the Mausoleum of Hadrian. His circular tomb, built in travertine and white marble, measured 210 feet in diameter and 66 feet tall. It was supported on a square base nearly 300 feet across and 40 feet high. And like the Mausoleum of Augustus, the top of the drum would have been planted with cypress trees.

The tomb was used for only sixty years. In 271 the tomb was included in the Aurelian Walls, thus beginning its extraordinary and varied history as a castle. It was to be the city's strongest fortress for more than one thousand years. In 847 it served as the residence and fortress for Pope Leo IV's Leonine City, whose walls enclosed the Vatican and Borgo district. This is where Clement VII wept as he watched his beautiful Villa Madama on the slopes of Monte Mario burn while he used the castle's artillery to discourage Charles V's army of thirty thousand troops from attacking the castle. Charles V's army turned from the castle to Rome and brought the entire city to its knees in 1527 with the Sack of Rome. The fortress then became a Renaissance prison and is now a museum.

Castel Sant'Angelo is by far the most popular sight in the city among the Romans. Like the Tower of London, its sinister history and tales of blood-curdling events over eighteen centuries provide an irresistible

Castel Sant' Angelo

attraction for young and old alike. The entrance to the museum is the door to the original tomb. From here we begin our climb upward in the shadowy interior. The most dramatic part of the climb is on Alexander VI's *cordonata*, which is in midair. Thank goodness the original rickety wooden draw-bridge has been replaced. At this point we are crossing the central burial chamber of Hadrian's tomb.

Many interesting and surprising things await us inside. We can see the prisons of San Marocco, where the Italian artist Benvenuto Cellini, as he tells us in his autobiography, was lowered by rope into a cell so small that he could hardly lie down. These cells were originally ventilation shafts. In the Cortile dell'Angelo is the facade of the Chapel of Leo X, one of Michelangelo's least-known works. The loggias by Antonio da Sangallo the Younger and Bramante frame superb views of Rome and Monte Mario. These loggias contain an Italian bar, an excellent place for a light lunch. In the Camera dei Festoni (Room of the Feast) hangs a painting that shows Cardinal Gozzadini receiving the Old Pretender (James Francis Edward Stuart) at Imola in 1717. The Old Pretender had fled to Imola after his unsuccessful attempt to reclaim the Scottish throne from England in 1715. And in the core of the building is the Sala della Biblioteca, the magnificent library, where up until 1870 the papal treasure was kept.

At the end of our climb we discover a narrow Roman stair leading to the terrace, whose panorama is guarded by a beautiful bronze angel, the Archangel Michael. According to legend, the Archangel Michael hovered above the summit of the Mausoleum sheathing his sword in a gesture of peace. Archangel Michael's revelation to the Pope's enormous procession, held to implore God's pardon, immediately ended the plague of 590, which had decimated the population of Rome.

From here we have a decision to make. How will we approach St. Peter's? We have two choices. Our first choice is the Via della Concilia-zione, a street lined with twenty-eight obelisks to mark the way. This is the street where, in 1934, Mussolini leveled the entire area between Bernini's colonnade and the Tiber. Mussolini destroyed the homes of more than five thousand people in this area to give St. Peter's an approach "worthy of the Temple of Christianity." Our second choice is to take the

Borgo Sant'Angelo and the Via dei Corridori, which form one continuous street running along the famous *passetto* (fortified corridor) that connects the castle to the Vatican. We select the latter, thus avoiding the mass of tourists and their convoys of buses. This decision allows us to arrive in the Piazza San Pietro as Bernini intended. Bernini's vast square is revealed dramatically, all at once, to all those who enter from this approach.

The enormous piazza is by far the most exceptional architectural space in the city. Bernini realized that the piazza not only had to frame the great basilica of St. Peter's, it also needed to provide a meeting place for the countless thousands of pilgrims who would gather here. He knew the piazza would serve as the intermediate ground between the church and the surrounding neighborhoods. Bernini's original plan for the square called for the completion of a third section of colonnade. This square was to belong to both the neighborhood and the church, with the massive rows of columns to intervene between the two. Look for the two round white stones set in the paving between the fountains and the obelisk— where CENTRO DEL COLONNATO is written—and stand there. The four rows of columns will magically disappear and just one row of columns will remain visible. This is the middle ground between the sacred and the profane.

The Archangel Michael

The Vatican

Based on the form of an ancient amphitheater, the piazza takes the shape of a colossal ellipse measuring nearly 790 feet wide. The surrounding colonnade is four rows deep and contains 284 huge Doric columns. On top of the colonnade, silhouetted against the sky, are 140 statues of the saints and various popes—the "vaults of heaven." In the center of the square is another Egyptian obelisk (nearly 92 feet tall). This obelisk is flanked on the right by Maderno's fountain and on the left by a fountain by Bernini. Bernini began work on the square in 1656, twenty-three years after completing the *baldacchino* inside the basilica, which he had begun at the unexpected age of twenty-five. He dedicated nine years to the *baldacchino* and another eleven years to the square.

The piazza is the quintessential example of Baroque architecture, particularly in its expression of the idea of movement and continuous change. All one needs to do is walk within the immense range of columns formed by the elliptical colonnades to appreciate the infinite variety of views, both within and without the colonnade. It is unfortunate that many visitors to St. Peter's first arrive by tour bus and are deprived of experiencing what is truly a work of genius.

The Colonnade

It is the work of Gian Lorenzo Bernini (1598–1680) that most profoundly changed the way we understand Rome today. Bernini realized that the Classical monuments and the new monumental work of his era had to coexist with the small houses and neighborhoods of the common people. With this in mind, Bernini designed the square at St. Peter's to blend into the surrounding city. Piazza San Pietro is placed on ground that slopes toward the Tiber and is partially hidden behind an open colonnade. This setting gives us veiled views into the neighborhoods next to the square and an open vista off into the city. Bernini intended to guide us by the dome of St. Peter's and to lead us from Ponte Sant'Angelo through the humble houses of the Borgo district right up to the facade of the great church. He intended for us to enter the interior of St. Peter's and then be guided by the light streaming down from the dome to the *baldacchino* placed under the vast space beneath. Marking the end of this procession, the "gloria"—the gilded bronze throne of St. Peter—is placed in the *apse*.

The scholar Leonardo Benevolo clearly understands Bernini's genius when he states, "In this way the face of modern Rome became fixed: a city that did not try to relive its past, but acted as guardian of its ancient remains, having learned to live alongside these reminders of a bygone age in a perfectly natural way."

St. Peter's is the most famous church in all of Christendom and the most sacred place of pilgrimage for Catholics. Between A.D. 64 and 67, St. Peter was martyred in the Circus of Nero on the Vatican Hill and then buried nearby. The current high altar is said to be built over the actual spot of the saint's tomb. In 1940 an entire Roman necropolis was discovered below the altar, verifying this ancient belief.

Julius II, the nephew of Sixtus IV, was elected Pope in 1503. Soon afterward he persuaded the architect Giuliano da Sangallo to move to Rome from Florence. He was then able to bring two of the most important artists of this generation, Michelangelo and Raphael, to Rome.

Julius II at first wanted Michelangelo to sculpt his tomb, which was to be placed in St. Peter's. While Michelangelo was working on the tomb, the Pope decided to completely rebuild St. Peter's to the design of Bramante, thus concentrating all available resources on this project. In

St. Peter's

1508, as part of the rebuilding project, the Pope asked Michelangelo (who was not entirely pleased about the decision to stop work on the tomb) and Raphael to paint two series of frescoes illustrating the world's cultural patrimony that would be both religious and humanistic. Both men created equally famous works: Michelangelo's Sistine Chapel and Raphael's Stanza.

Bramante began to work in 1505 on the St. Peter's we see today. The project began with the demolition of the old church to make way for the construction of a new St. Peter's. Bramante's destruction was so ruthless that he became known as "Mastro Ruinante" (Master of Destruction). His design for the church was laid out on a Greek plan, where all the spaces are generated outward from the dome. When Bramante died in 1514, Raphael, then Peruzzi, and then Antonio da Sangallo the Younger (who revised the design to a Latin cross) took over. To quote James Ackerman (the author of *The Architecture of Michelangelo*, 1986), "Almost every major architect in sixteenth-century Rome had a hand in the designing of St. Peter's." Eventually Michelangelo was called upon in 1546 to salvage the mess, and, at seventy-one years of age, Michelangelo only reluctantly agreed to do the work. His conditions to Paul III were that he would have a free hand with the design, and, in turn, he would work gratis until his death. Michelangelo then demolished all of Sangallo's work, except the crossing arches for the dome, and returned to Bramante's first principles. Michelangelo himself wrote, "One cannot deny that Bramante was as worthy an architect as any in ancient times. He laid down the first plan of St. Peter's, not full of confusion, but clear and pure, full of light . . . and it was regarded as a beautiful thing." This was the ultimate compliment, paid to one of his greatest rivals.

In 1607 Carlo Maderno won the competition to extend the *nave* of the church and add a new loggia and facade. Carlo Maderno's additions to Michelangelo's church returned the plan of the church to a Latin cross mostly for liturgical reasons. Although Maderno's facade is beautiful, it is criticized because it obscures the dome. The steps that lead to the Basilica are Bernini's. Although we have seen many other contributions to St. Peter's, Ackerman says, "The Basilica today owes more to Michelangelo than to any other architect." The construction of this church took 120 years, at a cost to the papacy of much more than the price of architects, building supplies, and teams of workmen. The collection of funds for the Basilica was, in fact, the spark which lit the fire of the Lutheran reform. This fire of reform split the church and unleashed the religious wars, eventually causing the break between Rome and the Church of England.

By now we know the celebrated works collected at St. Peter's: the famous interior of the great Basilica, the fifteenth-century central doors with the Ethiopian monks flanked by the two great equestrian statues— Bernini's *Constantine* and Cornacchini's *Charlemagne*. We know of the frescoes by Giotto, which were rescued from the old Basilica, and we know of Michelangelo's stunning *Pièta*, now protected against vandalism behind bulletproof glass. We can see that over the high altar is Bernini's *baldacchino*, which is forty-nine feet tall and made from the bronze beams taken from the portico of the Pantheon. We know of Canova's *Monument to the Last Stuarts*—a monument to the Roman Catholic claimants to the British throne exiled in Rome and buried here below us: James (the Old Pretender), Henry, and Charles (Bonnie Prince Charlie). And we know of the moving light, which comes streaking in from the lantern above in the giant dome. This light is especially brilliant when it falls on the face of St. Veronica, standing in her niche in one of the main pillars.

The interior is enormous. St. Peter's was built as the setting for great festivals and celebrations. It is a massive room where gold and marble serve as the backdrop for the shining halberds and helmets of the Swiss Guard as they flash about in their orange-and-purple-striped uniforms designed by Michelangelo. Probably the least conspicuous and possibly one of the most historically interesting objects is in the floor of the central *nave* near the entrance. Here is the great circular porphyry slab, where on Christmas Eve of the year 800 Charlemagne knelt for his coronation as the Emperor of the West.

Let's turn our eyes upward to the great dome. When Michelangelo died, only the drum was complete. Intending to emulate Brunelleschi's dome in Florence, Giacomo della Porta modified the dome's design and increased its height. To reach the lantern of the dome we must undertake a serious climb. Most of the journey is in the narrow space between the inner and outer walls of the dome. This climb is not for the faint of heart or those who suffer from claustrophobia. Once the ascent is completed, the 360-degree view of Rome is simply breathtaking!

To the east we can see the Piazzale Napoleone I, in front of the gardens of the Pincio, rising above the Piazza del Popolo. For Romans, evening is the classic hour for a stroll on the Pincio. The vast tree-covered hill beyond is the Villa Borghese, the first great Roman park villa. In the distance to the south is the district EUR (Esposizione Universale di Roma). Nervi's Palazzo dello Sport stands on the top of the hill, presiding over the formality of modern town planning and an array of dispassionate government buildings, including the Palazzo della Civiltà del Lavoro (the "Square

Colosseum") built during the Fascist era. And just beyond Monte Mario to the north lies Foro Mussolini, now Foro Italico—the Modern sports complex. This complex was begun in the 1920s when the architect Enrico del Debbio designed the Marble Stadium, ringed by sixty Classical statues of athletes, each representing one of Italy's provinces. Another stadium, the huge Olympic Stadium, was built for the 1960 Olympic Games and is capable of holding a hundred thousand spectators. In the foreground is Prati (Fields), named for the gardens and vineyards that covered the area until the end of the last century. Now this is a fashionable residential area with one of the best shopping districts in Rome, where along the Via Cola di Rienzo all manner of shops can be found. Some of my favorites in this area include Franchi, a delicatessen that makes the best seafood salad; Castroni, which sells its own coffee and a full selection of imported foods; and, of course, Pignotti, makers of excellent ice cream. From here we can see how much of the city is made up of gardens hidden behind their protective walls that line the streets. Besides these distant views, the elegant Vatican Gardens and the piazza, full of tour buses, can be seen just below. Very little of Rome escapes the watchful eye of this great dome.

EUR

Foro Italico

Much of my time this afternoon is spent in the Vatican Museum, contemplating the magnificent work of Raphael and Michelangelo. Sitting in the Stanze di Raffaello (Raphael's Rooms) I am struck by the frescoes painted by the then twenty-six-year-old Raphael. I linger in the Sistine Chapel to take time enough to absorb this superb fresco. It was painted in four years by the reluctant Michelangelo, who painted unassisted what was

described by Goethe as "the most sublime example of what one man is capable." If I were able to have my own way, I would close the Sistine Chapel to all but myself for my visit and have my flow of emotions not be interrupted by those who are less contemplative.

With special permission from the docents stationed near the entry to the stairs, we find the private spiral stair of Bramante with forty

columns spinning upward: Doric, Ionic, Corinthian, then Composite—the Roman order. This quiet stair is hidden away, somewhat ordinary, and constructed from only humble materials. After we view the art of an overwhelming number of important artists whose works are collected in the Vatican Museums, it is time for our appointment to visit the Vatican Gardens. (See the Information Office to the left of the portico in the front of the Basilica for an appointment time.)

The various palaces and the grottoes of the Vatican are interesting. Bramante's Belvedere, at 985 feet long, is amazing. What I want to see, though, is the body of the great Basilica. I want to see the rest of Michelangelo's church—the part that can be viewed only from the gardens.

From the gardens we are able to see, firsthand, the full beauty and flowing lines of Michelangelo's design of the Basilica. The grandeur of the giant order pilasters recalls those of the Palazzo Senatorio on the Capitol. We can see from the great bulk of the wall that the internal space is carved into the walls and not merely enclosed by them. Here we can see the walls wrap around the great Basilica, pierced by exquisite deep windows that Michelangelo's friend, the architect Giorgio Vasari, described as being "of varied form and awesome grandeur." Again we see that Michelangelo didn't think about the design; he felt the design intuitively. Our trip to St. Peter's is now complete.

St. Peter's

Day Trips

There are two places worth visiting: Tivoli, where the Villa d'Este and Villa Adriana (Hadrian's Villa) are located, and Ostia Antica, which is near the sea.

Tivoli

To reach Tivoli from Rome, take the blue line of the Metro to Rebibbia at the end of the line. Directly in front of the Metro station is the main stop for the blue ACOTRAL buses—stop A—where we can catch the bus to Tivoli. The hour-long ride through Rome's suburbs and then the Italian countryside is the perfect contrast to the busy city left behind. As we begin to rise above the valley, winding our way through the hills that surround Rome, we can catch glimpses back to the city and across the open countryside of the Tiburtine, dotted with small farmhouses, vineyards, and olive groves. The final approach to the little hill town is narrow and winding, just barely wide enough for the bus to pass. After this twisting climb, we reach Largo Garibaldi, the main square of Tivoli. The square is enclosed on three sides by shops and cafés. The fourth side is open, and we can see the entire valley below and, in the background, Rome. Largo Garibaldi has been nicknamed the "Balcony over Rome" by the locals. This is not the typical town square that we would find in Rome. Largo Garibaldi is a beau-

tiful tree-covered garden, complete with fountains and a reflecting pool
Just to the north, next to the magazine kiosk, is the bus stop for the local
orange CAT buses. From here the Villa Adriana bus will take us to Hadrian's vast Villa, just about three miles out of town.

Villa Adriana

Hadrian's Villa

It is still early in the morning. The air is fresh and cool, the sky is clear, and we are standing at one of the most evocative sites in Italy—Hadrian's Villa. In A.D. 118 the Emperor Hadrian began work on his enormous villa, spread over nearly thirty acres. Hadrian, the Emperor of the humanistic empire, was a lover of beauty, culture, and the arts. He loved poetry and

literature; he understood mathematics. He could both paint and sculpt and claimed to know all there was to know about peace and war. The art on which he focused his attention and to which he dedicated most of his energy was architecture. We have already seen the Mausoleum of Hadrian and the Pantheon, and now we stand in the midst of his vast Villa, which covers the hills around us. Taking ten years to build and covering an area equal to that of the center of Imperial Rome, it is Hadrian's masterpiece.

The Villa is not one building, nor a group of buildings collected about a shared garden or court. Hadrian gives us what is unique for its time: an assembly of buildings placed in what appears to be a haphazard manner among the hills. The buildings were then connected by covered walkways. If we look carefully we see that the buildings are placed so they harmonize with the site on which they stand, taking advantage of the terrain and the view. The vistas and movement created from the carefully positioned

Villa Adriana

buildings allow us to experience both the Villa and its gardens as well as the surrounding countryside. Though the Villa has been robbed of the art collected here, and the marble that once covered the walls is now gone, there is still plenty remaining to remind us of the grandeur that was the largest and most lavish villa ever built in the Roman Empire.

Hadrian was inspired by the countless places he traveled to as the emperor of the Roman Empire. Here we find the influence of elegant Greek art and rich, heavy Egyptian architecture. Hadrian remembered his own roots by constructing colorful Spanish buildings. He even copied a heating system invented by the Nordic people. This is now a place where many peaceful hours can be spent wandering among the ruins.

A visit to the Villa begins at the Poikile — an immense square with a reflecting pool enclosed by a giant wall. On axis from the Poikile and placed in a little valley is the most picturesque feature of the Villa, the Canopus. Its namesake, Canopus, is a small town in Egypt west of the Nile Delta. Canopus was connected by a canal to Alexandria, which was fifteen miles away. The Egyptian Canopus was made famous by the Sanctuary of Serapis and its grand festivals and banquets. Hadrian's design reflects the grandeur of the original. Here we find the canal — a long reflecting pool — lined with columns and statues that are copied from the temple dedicated to Serapis. At the end of the pool, ending the axis, is a large nymphaeum, or summerhouse, with a semicircular alcove used as a dining room for summer banquets. This setting, with its cool breezes coming off the pool and the noise from bubbling fountains and waterfalls, would have provided the Emperor with a shaded retreat for entertaining his guests.

Among the many various parts of the Villa, the Natatorium, or Maritime Theater, is undoubtedly the most interesting. It is a large (140 feet in diameter) circular building that contains a moat surrounding a small island. The island is the site of a miniature villa, complete with a hall, reception room, and a bathroom. When Hadrian wanted to get away from the court, he crossed over to the island, raised two wooden drawbridges, and completely isolated himself. This island villa was Hadrian's refuge from his duties as Emperor of the Roman Empire; this was where he came to enjoy solitude and to study.

Villa d'Este

Tivoli is a wonderful place to explore. Originally Tivoli was named Tibur after the legendary Tiburtus. Tivoli's history lies around every corner. Near the arched Ponte Lucano, the bridge where we cross the Aniene River to reach Tivoli, thirty-thousand-year-old human remains have been discovered. Along the Via Campitelli we find a dense medieval neighborhood clinging to the side of the hill. Where the ancient temple to Hercules once stood now stands the Duomo, the Cathedral of St. Lorenzo. Inside the Cathedral is the *Deposition* — a group of rare wood carvings from the thirteenth century — and the exquisite baptismal spring and the sacristy designed by Bernini, which includes a sculpture of Jesus being baptized. High on a hill, overlooking the entire town, looms Pope Pius II's Renaissance fortress — Rocca Pia — with its four massive cylindrical towers. We also discover the ruins of the once elegant Temple of Vesta, the goddess of earth and fire, and the Temple of Sibyl. At the beginning of the millennium the Sibyl, Tiburtina, was believed to have predicted the birth of Christ. In the Piazza Trento is nestled the fifth-century church of Santa Maria Maggiore. We arrive, stand in front of the church's Gothic portal, and witness the end of a wedding ceremony. To our right is a modest archway: the entrance to the Villa d'Este.

Cardinal Ippolito asked the architect Pirro Ligorio to design the magnificent sixteenth-century Villa d'Este. Here we can stroll among fantastic fountains in an extraordinary Italian garden. The Cardinal's guests would have arrived at the entrance at the foot of the hill, moved up through the garden passing hundreds of fountains, and reached the ceremonial staircase. The guests would then climb the stairs to reach a wide terrace overlooking the entire garden and the countryside beyond. On this terrace is where the imposing Villa stands. Today we arrive through a series of courtyards, hallways, and beautiful frescoed rooms to reach the terrace with its panorama spreading before us. The frescoes are the work of many great artists, including Federico Zuccari and Girolamo Muziano. Pirro Ligorio designed the garden, including more than five hundred fountains. He also designed the canal system that brings water from the Aniene River to the Villa, and the timing devices that operated the fountains. Ligorio

Villa d' Este

designed these devices to trigger the fountains to spring up suddenly and spray unsuspecting guests.

One of the fountains not designed by Ligorio is the *Fontana del Bicchierone* (Fountain of the Large Drinking Glass). Bernini's simple fountain is a giant seashell containing a fine chalice. Overgrown by the garden, the beautiful curved form of the chalice and the single spout of water give a poetic contrast to the roar of the famous Avenue of a Hundred Fountains.

The garden is slightly neglected and overgrown, and many of the fountains are in need of repair. This is a place of melancholy beauty. This beauty is best found in the *Fontana dell'Ovato* (Egg-shaped Fountain) located at the end of the Avenue of a Hundred Fountains. Placed in between an outcropping of rocks, surrounded by a grove of trees, this fountain was designed by Pirro Ligorio to receive the water brought from the Aniene. This Baroque fountain is a wonderful blend of architecture, sculpture, rocks, and plants. The principal feature of the fountain is the statue *Sybil of Tibur*, by Flemish Giglio della Vellita, which sits among the trees and rocks above the fountain. She is holding the hand of a cherub that represents Tivoli. Half-buried in the rocks below her, one on each side, are two marble effigies representing the rivers of Tivoli, the Aniene and the Herculanean. We take the half-hidden path that loops around the fountain to find the Fountain of Pegasus. Intended to be seen rising above the Sybil, the little winged horse is all but overgrown, and in the dappled light of early evening it takes on an almost surreal quality.

By day the gardens offer a wonderful place for a lazy walk. They are cool, shady, and peaceful. At night we find an entirely different place. Where by day there was only water, by night we have both light and water. This interplay between light and water produces ethereal effects.

Ostia Antica

Ostia Antica is an hour from Rome and can be easily reached by train. Ostia Antica, Rome's seaport, originally sat on the coast of the Tyrrhenian Sea. The Tiber ran alongside the northern edge of the ancient city. According to legend this is where Aeneas, the forefather of the Latins, landed in the seventh century B.C. and established a settlement. By the end of the first century A.D. Ostia had become a rich and prosperous town. Its population of more than fifty thousand inhabitants was a mix of sailors, merchants, craftsmen, and state officials, as well as workers and transporters. As a port city Ostia had two major drawbacks: the facility was too small, and the silt from the river continually clogged the waterway. To remedy this, Emperor Claudius, in the middle of the first century A.D., constructed a new port to the north of the mouth of the river. Claudius' new port continued to fill with silt from the river, requiring Emperor Trajan to build new docks several miles to the northwest, where the airport at Fiumicino is now located.

Pompeii, Herculaneum, and Ostia remain as they were in Roman times. Ostia is the only example of an urban center from the Imperial era. Here we come face-to-face with the daily life of those who lived here two thousand years ago.

The sea has receded, and the river now flows in a new course. There have been wars, malaria, and floods. The atmosphere here is heavy. We walk on the old paving stones where ruins of ancient brick walls hide under masses of ivy, broken columns form the skyline, and elegant parasol pines protect us from the sun.

It is best to arrive in Ostia early. There are innumerable streets to wander and an entire city to explore. At the House of the Charioteers we discover a two-story-high arcade and well-preserved impressionistic paintings of horses pulling their chariots, painted in soft natural hues. In the commercial quarter near the river is Horrea Epagathiana, whose elegant porch provides a model for the many doorways and window surrounds of Rome's Renaissance palazzi. At the Bath of the Seven Sages we see a beautiful black and white mosaic floor depicting a variety of hunting scenes intertwined with decorative plants. On the Decumanus, the main street of Ostia, we find the fishmonger's shop, where in the shade of the parasol pines the thick marble tables for displaying the fish still stand. The figures of a dolphin and a squid are depicted in the shop's black and white mosaic floor. Near the amphitheater is the bakery, which still has its ancient mills made of lavic stone. Just before the House of Diana is a thermopolium, where hot drinks were served. The serving counter and the shelves for bottles, as well as a basin for washing dishes, still exist. And probably the most intact building is the House of Diana, a multistory hotel complete with a communal toilet. To contrast the hotel, the House of the Fortuna Annonaria is one of the richest houses in Ostia. The house has a large tree-filled courtyard with travertine columns. The rooms of the house have splendid marble floors under which hot air circulates to heat the room. This is only a small glimpse of what is waiting to be discovered at Rome's ancient seaport.

Ostia Antica

Ostia Antica

Ancient Rome

The Roman Forum and the Palatine

In 1922 Benito Mussolini marched on Rome. This marked the beginning of more than twenty-two years of Fascist rule. Mussolini, more than any other dictator of the time, chose to express himself with the new Modern architecture that was sweeping Europe, stating that "It would be unthinkable not to be in favor of the rational and functional architecture of our time." His dream was to restore Rome as the *caput mundi* (head of the world) or at least head of the Latin bloc of states.

On December 31, 1925, Mussolini outlined his intentions for a town-planning policy based on the idea of grandeur. This policy was meant to establish a connection between the Roman Empire and Fascism. The principal accomplishment of this policy, during the twenty-two years of Fascism, was to connect the Colosseum with the Piazza Venezia by the Via dei Fori Imperiali—an act that earned Mussolini the nickname "His Majesty the Pickaxe." Palaces were torn down, hills were leveled, streets and squares were wiped out, and the ancient ruins of Rome were paved over. During the Via dei Fori Imperiali's construction, three hundred ninety-three thousand cubic yards of earth were moved and more than six hundred apartments destroyed, displacing nearly two thousand people. The Imperial Forums were the worst casualties of this grand scheme. The historian Henry Hope Reed called it the "Third Sack of Rome"!

By the end of the first century B.C. the Roman Forum could no longer accommodate its population of four hundred thousand inhabitants. The only ground available for expansion was the area of the lower-class district to the east, along the slopes of the Quirinal. Since the expropriation of land for public use was prohibited, the land had to be purchased at market value. In 54 B.C. Julius Caesar bought the land behind the Curia for sixty million *sestertiums*, an astronomical sum, and built the first new forum, the Forum of Caesar. This single act provided two important precedents. First, it provided a way to expand the city center, a precedent followed by the construction of the Imperial Forums of Augustus, Nerva, Vespasian, and Trajan. This was the first time Rome had extended itself since ancient times. Second, and more important, was the ideological consequence. By giving his own name to the new forum, Caesar demonstrated a dramatic shift in the power structure of Rome. The days of the Republic were numbered, and within just a few years Imperial Rome would emerge, and the Emperor Augustus would be raised to the level of a god.

Very little now remains of these once great forums. Except for Trajan's column, which has stood "firm in its pristine majesty," most of what is left are only broken columns and "wistful piles of stone." Alongside Trajan's Forum, that mighty group of buildings climbing up the hill, is Trajan's Market. Built by Apollodorus of Damascus at the beginning of the second century A.D., it shored up the collapsing hill and provided Rome with its finest market. The principal feature of the market is the great exedra that faces the forum. Inside the market is a multistory structure of covered corridors lined with 150 individual shops. Every time I visit here I wonder if this was the world's first shopping mall.

Before we enter the Roman Forum, the center of the Roman Republic city life, let's try to picture what must have been here nearly thirty centuries ago. In the tenth century B.C., scattered across the seven hills along the southern bank of the Tiber, there were only small villages of farmers and shepherds. The valleys between were marshy and only used as

Trajan's Market

burial grounds. Between the Palatine and the Capitoline Hills in the marshy lowlands below was one such cemetery, probably belonging to the Iron Age village that then existed on the summit of the Palatine. This cemetery, along a muddy road, was known as the forum (from the word that meant "outside the walls"). This area became the marketplace and common ground for the early tribes that lived in the surrounding area. The legendary war with the Sabines of the Quirinal, touched off by the rape of their women, ended in 753 B.C. when peace was concluded in the forum by Romulus, the first king of Rome. As soon as peace emerged, the development of the forum began. The first Romans were of pastoral and farming stock—men who counted their wealth by head of cattle and made offerings of milk to their gods. They were deeply religious people who recognized the mysterious power of the world around them, which they named and embodied. One god was Jupiter, God of the Sky and Sunlight; another was Mars, Spirit of the Fields and later the God of War. Religion belonged to all aspects of their everyday life. The early Romans were a sober, purposeful people, who believed in discipline, industry, and frugality, and had a great sense of community spirit. When the Cloaca Maxima—the extraordinary drainage system to drain the water from the valley into the Tiber—was completed, sometime around 600 B.C., the cemetery and the adjacent huts beside the Via Sacra were demolished, and a gravel pavement was laid down over the remains.

The first identifiable sites in the Roman Forum were social and religious in nature: the Comitium, the public meeting place, and the Vulcanal, the Altar of Vulcan. Soon to follow were the Regia, the seat of the chief priest; the Temple of Vesta, where the sacred flame (the symbol of Rome's continuity) burned day and night tended by the Vestals; and the Curia, the official meeting place of the Senate. The Via Sacra (Sacred Way), Rome's most ancient street, was the main street of the Forum. As the power of Rome grew, so did the Forum. Eventually the Forum's first basilica, Basilica Aemilia, was built. The Basilica Giulia—where Mark Anthony made his famous speech after Caesar's murder—and a variety of temples would be constructed and were visible evidence of the city's growing wealth.

The basilicas were the places where people gathered and conducted business, and they had an important role in everyday Roman life. Basically the Roman basilicas were great halls with one or two aisles defined by rows of columns running alongside a central space, the *nave*, which had a higher ceiling and was lit from above by clerestory windows. Porticos usually lined one or more sides of the building connecting the great hall to an open colonnade, which was the favorite place of the famous Roman money changers. Later basilicas developed one or more *apses* in the side or end walls, the room from where the emperor exercised his power in public. The name "basilica" is Greek, and some eminent scholars tell us that the building was inspired by the Greek peristyles. The Roman basilica has a similar plan but a higher ceiling than its Greek counterpart. My guess is that the airless heat of summer in Rome required another building type with a greater volume to provide a cool place to retreat in the heat of midday.

The basilica is one of the Roman contributions to architecture, serving as the model for the Christian churches that would follow some centuries later. Ultimately a dome emerged on these churches, transforming the Roman basilica further, giving us the great domed churches we see today.

The Temple of Antoninus and Faustina is raised on a huge platform, only to be reached by a distinctive flight of steps. Unlike their counterparts in Greece, which sat close to the ground, Roman temples were raised to give them an air of dignity.

Standing amongst the ruins is the Arch of Septimius Severus. Like the basilica, the triumphal arch is another particularly Roman work of architecture. Of the many arches that once stood in Rome, only three survive today in anything like their original state. The influence of these three arches, though, has been widespread and is obvious in the Marble Arch in London and the Arc de Triomphe in Paris. The imperial palace in Berlin even has a replica of the Arch of Septimius Severus as its entrance.

Among the broken columns and the oleanders we find the Via Sacra and the square that was the Forum proper. The modern Italian piazza is a direct descendent of the ancient Forum and has a similar role in the

Forum

city today as it did in classical times. It has been said that the reason Italians pay so little attention to the interior of their houses and, like the ancient Romans, have the smallest bedrooms is that they have the largest and finest of all living rooms—the piazza. In republican times the square was the center of every aspect of the city's life: great religious ceremonies took place there, along with triumphal marches, sacrifices, and funeral processions. Court was held there in full sight of the citizens. Even the early gladiatorial games were held in the square. The Forum was the meeting place for everyone.

Today the once great Forum, whose permanent residents are hundreds of "Forum cats," is a vast empty space with grass growing among the paving stones. A few columns stand as sentinels to remind us of what must have been.

At the head of the Via Sacra, marking the entrance to the Forum, stands the Arch of Titus. Taking the little path to the right—the Clivus Palatinus, which is still paved with original stones in some places—we begin to ascend a hill. Sunlight filtering through the trees, dark shade all around, we are rising above the Forum. We are climbing to the summit of the Palatine, the only place in the city where we can still see a Classical landscape with ruins. The Palatine derives its name from the Latin word *palatium*, which means the "center of power." The Palatine Hill has given its name to all the other palaces of the world, and it was the first of the original Seven Hills to be inhabited, predating the site of the Roman Forum. This was the cradle of Roman civilization. Rising more than two hundred feet above the Tiber and the Isola Tiberina below, the hill not only occupied a key strategic site, it also enjoyed cool breezes from the sea in the hot summer months that would make it a prime place to live for the next millennium. This is the hill where Romulus and Remus were suckled by the she-wolf. And in 753 B.C. the first boundaries for the developing city were drawn, the *Roma Quadrata*.

The hill became the most favored place to live when the most important citizens of the city began to build their homes there, including Agrippa, Cicero, Tiberius, and Domitian. Augustus was born on the hill. Domitian had the most ambitious building program, building two palaces with an adjacent stadium. As the Palatine grew, the Forum shrank. The Palatine remained the official place of residence for the emperor into the Middle Ages. In the sixteenth century Cardinal Alessandro Farnese had the great Renaissance architect Giacomo da Vignola design the beautiful Farnese Gardens, which were laid over the ruins.

In our mind's eye we have all been here before. We are standing in the midst of a landscape painting by Poussin or Claude Lorrain. The hill and gardens look very much today as they must have looked then. It is easy to understand, by simply wandering among the ancient remains, why for 250 years, beginning in the sixteenth century, Paul Brill and the other Flemish artists painted their many small pictures of Classical ruins. It was from these paintings, and the enlightened taste of eighteenth-century English travellers who purchased them, that the designers of the English landscape garden drew their inspiration. These images of the ruined Palatine forever changed the English countryside into picturesque landscapes where the English garden designers placed replicas of Classical ruins and temples among dark groves of trees that were reflected in tranquil waters.

Even for those without any special archaeological training the hill is a wonderful place to roam and soak up the atmosphere. Sit among fallen columns along the belvedere and look down on the giant Circus Maximus. The Circus Maximus in its day could hold three hundred thousand spectators watching as many as twenty-four chariot races a day. The races would last as long as fifteen days. Today the hill is more of a contemplative place, where orange trees, oleander, and groves of cypress line the paths that wind among the ancient stones. Rising just behind the Circus is the Aventine Hill, where Giambattista Piranesi, the famous engraver, designed the Piazza dei Cavalieri di Malta in the second half of the eighteenth century. And on the horizon loom the massive Baths of Caracalla, once the most luxurious baths in all of Rome. The Baths of Caracalla are now the venue for eccentric summer opera performances.

It is nearing sunset. We promised ourselves that we would conclude our visit to ancient Rome with a visit to the Colosseum, that "noble wreck in ruinous perfection" (Byron), in the light of the waning sun. It is just below us through the pine trees. Winding our way among the ruins,

The Palatine Hill

retracing our steps, we return to the Arch of Titus at the bottom of the hill. This time we turn to our right. Just at the bottom of the hill, marking the head of the Via Sacra, is the Arch of Constantine. Designed to honor Constantine's victory over Maxentius at the Battle of Milvian Bridge, it is Rome's best-preserved triumphal arch and its largest. In front of the arch looms the massive Colosseum. We take one last look back at the Forum. From here one can see the whole length of the Forum with the Campidoglio as a backdrop—the classic photo opportunity. We take the Via Sacra, whose paving stones are still in place, past the Temple of Venus and Rome (designed by Hadrian and once the largest in Rome) to the Piazza del Colosseo.

Forum

Near the Arch of Constantine is a little country road, bordered by pines and an old stone wall, which leads us to an ancient church. If you follow the road all you need to do is ring the bell on the old gateway, then enter into one of the unexpected corners of this ancient hill. Very little has changed here since the tenth century. We enter a little garden filled with daffodils, lilies, violets, roses, masses of acanthus, and even a vine-covered trellis. All of this belongs to the quaint little chapel of San Sebastiano in Pallaria, with the house of the fortunate parish priest next to it. Just a little farther along the road is the church of San Bonaventura standing on the highest peak of the Palatine.

The Colosseum

Off and on as we have been wandering among the ruins of the Forum and the Palatine we have caught glimpses of the Colosseum along the skyline. And now we are finally going to explore the greatest remaining monument of classical Rome. A description of such a place should only be attempted in the still of the night, after midnight, when reality blurs in shadows and the images touch the heart.

When Michelangelo was working on the great basilica of St. Peter's he was found one wintry morning, after a heavy snowfall, wandering among the ruins of the vast Colosseum. He had come here to lift his soul, to find the inspiration required to guide and direct his own work. This is the power of simple beauty: the beauty that an arena can give a church.

The Colosseum was known in ancient times as the Flavian Amphitheater and was the work of three emperors of the Flavian dynasty. The Emperor Vespasian began work on the project in A.D. 72 with the help of twelve thousand Jewish slaves brought to Rome after the Judean revolt. His

Rome

son, Titus, inaugurated the arena in A.D. 80 with a celebration that included five thousand animals hunted and killed during one hundred days of continuous games. The Colosseum is the place where the policy of "bread and circuses" placated the citizens of Rome in Imperial times. Many of the common people lived parasitically off the Empire. Because of low living standards, high unemployment, and an unwillingness to work, the population was always on the verge of rebellion. The games in the Colosseum served as a great diversion from unemployment and secured the emperor's authority.

The enormous Flavian Amphitheater was built on the marshy land of the artificial lake next to Nero's Golden House. This land was taken back by Vespasian for the people of Rome. The design for the Amphitheater was inspired by the Theater of Marcellus. In "honor" of Nero, his colossal statue, made of marble and standing 110 feet tall, was placed near the arena, thus providing the name of Colosseo.

The plan of the building is a giant ellipse, measuring 187 feet high, 610 feet long, and 512 feet across. There was enough room inside to seat eighty-seven thousand spectators and to allow standing room for another twenty thousand. Eighty flights of stairs, the *vomitoria*, provided for quick exit (within three minutes) in times of danger. Along the top of the upper story a huge canvas awning (the *velarium*), supported by 240 masts, was stretched across the arena by sailors from the Imperial fleet to protect the spectators from the sun. The most famous detail is the columns half-embedded in the walls on the exterior arcades. These are Doric on the ground level, Ionic on the second level, and Corinthian on the third level, and on the uppermost level is a wall supported by Corinthian pilasters with a small window in every other space. In the spaces between were placed the now vanished bronze shields of Domitian, who put the finishing touches on the arena. This beckoned Byron to write in *Childe Harold*,

> Arches on arches! as it were that Rome,
> Collecting the chief trophies of her line,
> Would build up all her triumphs in one dome,
> Her Colosseum stands . . .

The Colosseum

The Colosseum was built almost entirely of blocks of travertine, not a particularly fine stone, full of holes like tufa (volcanic rock). The stone was quarried in Tivoli, and the color of the stone ranged between white and yellow. One can imagine how beautiful the arena, and for that matter all the monuments in Rome, would be if the builders had had at their disposal the fine sandstone used in Lyon or Edinburgh. Even so, the work here is beautiful. Each joint between the immense travertine blocks shows how carefully they were placed.

The *podium* was the place reserved for the Vestals, the senators, the chief magistrates, and of course the emperor and his family. When I stand in this place of honor I am so close to the arena that I would be able to clearly see the smallest detail of battle and the facial expressions of the dying gladiators.

Borgia Stairs

Basilica di
San Clemente

Santi Quattro Coronati

Santi Quattro Coronati

This remarkable structure was much admired by the Renaissance architects who found inspiration for the loggias of the Palazzo Venezia, for the courtyard of the Palazzo Farnese, and probably for the facade of the Palazzo Cancelleria. It has served as a model for large stadiums ever since.

Even all that was noteworthy about the Colosseum did not prevent it from being used as a quarry up into the eighteenth century. When Pope Pius VIII in the early 1800s finally began the preservation work, the once splendid arena had lost most of its outer wall and was overrun with vegetation. (Two books about the plant life of the Colosseum identify 420 species, some of which are exotic importations whose seeds were introduced with the animal fodder of classical times.) Like many other monuments in the city, this one too served as a stronghold in the eleventh and twelfth centuries. This stronghold belonged to the powerful Frangipane family. Eventually, after being damaged by a severe earthquake, it became a shelter for prostitutes as well as home for Rome's transient population. Thanks to Mussolini—who opened up the Via dei Fori Imperiali by wiping out the Imperial Forums and leveling the hill of the Velia to allow him to see the Colosseum from his windows in the Palazzo Venezia—today the great arena is ringed by Rome's infamous thundering traffic.

If you climb to the upper stories you can sit quietly and think about the ruins below. Or, if you like, you can scan the horizon for Rome's monuments. You can see San Pietro in Vincoli, the church famous for the tomb of Julius II and Michelangelo's *Moses*. The piazza in front of the church is where the sinister Borgia Stairs lead down to the Via Cavour. On the Oppian Hill you can see the remains of Nero's gigantic palace. To the south, rising above the roofs, is the ancient church of Santi Quattro Coronati and its fortified convent where, by ringing a bell, a nun will give you entry into a beautiful private courtyard. At the bottom of the hills is the Basilica of San Clemente, where in 1857 Father Mullooly, an Irish Dominican, began to unearth first a fourth-century church below the present one and then, below that, a Mithraic temple that is a full two levels below ground. This is the best-preserved archaeological site in Rome. And of course to the north you can see a panorama of the forums with the Campidoglio ending the vista.

Since early childhood this has been a place of memories for me. As I stand in these ancient ruins, their vastness fills me with emotion. This is one place on earth that has seen greatness.

The famous proverb declares that as long as the Colosseum stands, so will Rome; when Rome falls, so will the world.

The Colosseum

Rome